The Dorling Kindersley

ILLUSTRATED
FAMILY
ENCYCLOPEDIA

VOLUME 14 CONTENTS, STONE AGE – UNIVERSE

LONDON, NEW YORK, MUNICH,
MELBOURNE AND DELHI

Senior Editor Jayne Parsons   **Senior Art Editor** Gillian Shaw

Project Editors
Marian Broderick, Gill Cooling,
Maggie Crowley, Hazel Egerton,
Cynthia O'Neill, Veronica Pennycook,
Louise Pritchard, Steve Setford, Jackie Wilson

Project Art Editors
Jane Felstead, Martyn Foote,
Neville Graham, Jamie Hanson,
Christopher Howson, Jill Plank, Floyd Sayers,
Jane Tetzlaff, Ann Thompson

Editors
Rachel Beaugié, Nic Kynaston, Sarah Levete,
Karen O'Brien, Linda Sonntag

Art Editors
Tina Borg, Diane Clouting,
Tory Gordon-Harris

DTP Designers
Andrew O'Brien, Cordelia Springer

Managing Editor Ann Kramer   **Managing Art Editor** Peter Bailey

Senior DTP Designer Mathew Birch

Picture Research Jo Walton, Kate Duncan, Liz Moore

DK Picture Library Ola Rudowska, Melanie Simmonds

Country pages by PAGE*One*: Bob Gordon, Helen Parker,
Thomas Keenes, Sarah Watson, Chris Clark

Cartographers Peter Winfield, James Anderson

Research Robert Graham, Angela Koo

Editorial Assistants Sarah-Louise Reed, Nichola Roberts

Production Louise Barratt, Charlotte Traill

First published in Great Britain in 1997, 2004
by Dorling Kindersley Limited,
80 Strand, London WC2R 0RL

Copyright © 1997, © 2004 Dorling Kindersley Limited, London
A Penguin company

This edition published in 2004 by MDS BOOKS/MEDIASAT Group in association with MediaFund Limited

www.mediasatgroup.com

A CIP catalogue record for this book is available from the British Library

ISBN: 84 9789 537 1 (ISBN of the collection)
ISBN: 84 9789 534 7 (ISBN of this volume)
ISSN: 1744 2214

Not to be sold separately from the Daily Mail

Colour reproduction by Colourscan, Singapore
Printed and bound in the E.U.

STONE AGE

ABOUT TWO AND A HALF million years ago, human ancestors, or hominids, started to make and use basic stone tools, such as handaxes, for cutting and slicing. A million years later, hominids with larger brains, known as *Homo erectus* (upright people), made more complicated stone tools, such as arrowheads and small blades. This period is known as the Old Stone Age, or Palaeolithic Age. With these sharp tools, hominids carved bone and antlers, made clothes from animal skins, and chopped wood for fire and shelter. Later, in the Neolithic, or New Stone Age, humans created beautiful paintings and sculptures. In Europe, the period between the Old and New Stone Ages was called the Mesolithic, or Middle Stone Age.

Types of stone and bone tools

When ancient flintworkers realized they could predict the size and shape of flint chips coming off a flint core, they began to use the chips, or microliths, as blades, and then as arrowheads. This way of working has become known as the Levallois Technique. Tools became more specialized and people began to make stone knives and scrapers. They began to make tools of other materials – hammers, needles, and harpoons were made of antler or bone.

Handaxe
The sharp points and twin edges of handaxes made them useful for all sorts of chopping and cutting jobs, from butchering meat and making clothes, to cutting down branches for shelter.

Harpoon
Ancient people mounted bone harpoon heads on wooden shafts and used them to spear fish.

Rounded head of hammer

Antler hammer
An antler or bone hammer was used for hitting flint rocks and detaching small flakes, which could then be used as blades.

Scraper

Flint tools with one curved sharp edge could be used to prepare animal skins for clothing. People probably used this example more than 35,000 years ago.

Arrowhead

Hunters tied finely worked flint arrowheads to wooden shafts, to make useful weapons.

Point for boring holes

Sharp edge for cutting

Burin

This type of pointed tool could have been used for making engravings on cave walls. This burin is more than 35,000 years old.

Art and sculpture

Humans produced some superb paintings and sculptures in the Stone Age. Often, these works were made in deep, dark caves. Archaeologists think that they were decorations for special ceremonial centres or secret religious shrines used by Stone Age priests.

Portable art
An artist in France carved this stylized mammoth from an animal's shoulder blade more than 10,000 years ago. Artists often portrayed the quarry of the local hunters, hoping that this would bring them good luck when hunting. Mammoth meat was popular food.

In-situ sculpture
Sometimes sculptures were "built-in" to caves. These clay bison form the centrepiece of a small, low chamber in a cave at Tuc d'Audoubert, France.

Cave and rock painting
Some of the finest Stone Age paintings have been found in the caves of Europe and the rock shelters of Australia. This painting of hunters or warriors comes from Valltorta in Spain, and may be 10,000 years old.

Making a handaxe

Simple pebbles were the very first tools, but then Stone Age people learned to make better tools by striking one piece of stone against another, a process known as flint-knapping. They could then turn a core tool, like the one below, into a handaxe.

Core tool

Flintworkers first trimmed a suitable piece of flint into a core tool by striking it with a stone hammer, such as a quartzite pebble. The tool was then roughly the right shape to be worked into a handaxe.

Flake tool

The flintworkers learned to predict how the stone would break when sharply hit with the stone hammer. They then sliced off long flakes from the underside of the core tool. This gave the axe a sharp, strong edge.

Underside

Pressure flaking
The flintworker finished the axe by hitting its edge with a bone or antler hammer to remove small flakes of stone. This made it very sharp.

Crafts

People used clay, reeds, and wood to produce cooking and carrying utensils. Few wooden objects have survived, though a plank at least 50,000 years old has been discovered in Japan.

Pottery
The first pots were made in Japan 12,500 years ago by rolling clay into a long sausage shape and coiling it in a spiral. The sides of the vessel were then smoothed down.

Bowl

Basket-making
Stone Age people wove twigs, reeds, grass, and canes to make containers. Impressions of basketwork in ancient mud floors in western Asia show that baskets date back 10,000 years.

Basket

Timeline

2–2.5 million years BC Hominids start to use crude pebble tools.

1.3 million years BC Handaxes are developed, followed by finely shaped tools in Africa.

Handaxe

460,000 BC First evidence of hominids using fire, Zhoukoudian, China.

100,000 BC Modern humans evolve.

60,000 BC Flint-knapping spreads to Europe.

9000–8500 BC Neolithic Age begins in western Asia.

6500 BC Neolithic Age begins in Europe.

3000 BC Metal weapons and tools start to replace stone.

Microliths

FIND OUT MORE   ART, HISTORY OF   BRONZE AGE   CRAFTS   HUMAN EVOLUTION   PREHISTORIC PEOPLE

STORMS

TORRENTIAL RAIN, THUNDER, lightning, and gales can bring turmoil and devastation. To most of us, a storm is a spell of severe weather, with strong winds and heavy rain. Meteorologists – people who study the weather – define a storm as a wind blowing persistently at over 103–117 kmh (64–72.7 mph). Storms form in areas of low pressure, where air is warm and less dense than the surrounding air. In certain conditions, more powerful storms can develop. These are known as typhoons, cyclones, hurricanes, or Willy-Willy in different parts of the world.

Slice through a hurricane

Hurricanes

These huge storms can measure about 650 km (400 miles) in diameter. Hurricanes develop as clusters of thunderstorms over warm tropical seas. They tighten into a spiral, with a calm central ring of low pressure, called the eye. They sweep westward with heavy rain and winds up to 350 kmh (220 mph). As they pass over cool water or land, their intensity lessens.

Ice-crystals form on the top of the clouds.

Air billowing from the top of the storm causes the clouds to spread out.

The strongest winds are found beneath the eye wall, immediately outside the eye.

Eye wall

Air descends into the calm eye, leaving it free of cloud. Winds are less than 25 kmh (16 mph).

Winds in excess of 160 kmh (100mph) occur beneath the storm.

The heat contained by the warm sea provides the energy needed to drive the storm.

Spiral rain band

Warm, moist air spirals up around the eye inside the hurricane.

Hurricane damage

Violent winds cause the most hurricane damage, flattening whole buildings and uprooting trees. There may also be a sudden rise in sea-level, called a storm surge. This can bring widespread flooding. Hurricane Andrew in Florida, USA (above) killed 15 people and left over 50,000 homeless in 1992.

Tornadoes

Small but ferocious, tornadoes are whirling masses of wind spiralling beneath a thunder-cloud. They roar past in minutes, bringing winds of up to 400 kmh (250 mph) that leave a trail of destruction. Air pressure at the centre is so low that air rushes in at enormous speed, sucking up people, cars, and even whole trains.

Waterspouts

When a tornado passes over water, it sucks water up into a column called a waterspout. These usually develop over shallow water in summer. Waterspouts tend to last longer than tornadoes, but their wind speed is often less than 80 kmh (50 mph).

Dust devils

In deserts, there is so much loose, light, dusty material that tornadoes create columns of dust – dust devils. These are caused by columns of hot air whirling up, carrying debris from the ground.

Thunderstorms

Created from huge cumulonimbus clouds, thunderstorms bring heavy rain, thunder, and lightning. They are made by strong updraughts along a cold front or over ground warmed by summer sun. Air expanding quickly causes thunder, the rumbling that follows lightning.

Lightning

Air currents in a thunder-cloud hurl water drops together so violently that the cloud bristles with electrical charge, which is then unleashed in a dramatic flash of lightning.

Clement Wragge

Popular myth has it that the idea of naming hurricanes came from Australian Clement Wragge (1852–1922). It is said that he decided to give hurricanes the names of women he particularly disliked. Today, hurricanes are named according to an alphabetic list, created each year, of alternating men's and women's names.

 FIND OUT MORE | AIR | CLIMATE | CLOUDS | DESERTS | FRANKLIN, BENJAMIN | OCEANS AND SEAS | RAIN | WEATHER | WEATHER FORECASTING | WINDS

STRAVINSKY, IGOR

IGOR STRAVINSKY WAS probably the greatest composer of the 20th century. He was born in Russia in 1882, but later lived in Paris and the USA. He first found fame with *The Firebird*, a ballet based on old Russian stories. Much of his work had its roots in Russian traditional music, but it evolved throughout the composer's life as he changed his style to produce exciting and sometimes shocking musical effects.

Early life

Stravinsky was born near St. Petersburg, where his father was a singer. As a young man he trained as a lawyer, but, in 1902, he met the composer Rimsky-Korsakov and decided to devote his life to music. He studied with Rimsky-Korsakov, and the influence of the great Russian composers can be heard in his early music.

Ballets Russes

Stravinsky wrote three of his best-known works – *The Firebird*, *Petrushka*, and *The Rite of Spring* – for this ballet company, run by Russian impresario Diaghilev. Stravinsky was still a young man when he wrote these nationalistic Russian ballets, and they took Paris by storm. The success of *The Firebird* made Stravinsky famous all over the world.

Sergei Diaghilev

Diaghilev

Sergei Diaghilev (1872–1929) was an active promoter of the arts in his native Russia before moving to Paris in 1908. The following year he founded the Ballets Russes, which commissioned music by the young Stravinsky and other notable composers to accompany the dancers.

The Rite of Spring

This ballet tells the story of a sacrificial maiden dancing herself to death. Its jagged rhythms and violent harmonies were too much for some of the audience at the first performance. Fights broke out between those for and against the music, and the ballet ended in chaos. The piece launched modernism in music.

Characters from *The Rite of Spring*

Firebird

Stravinsky's first score for the Ballets Russes, *The Firebird*, was first performed in 1910. The Russian story suited Stravinsky's colourful orchestral style. Although he lived in Western Europe, Stravinsky still wrote music on Russian themes.

Brightly coloured costumes were a hallmark of the Ballets Russes.

Costume design for The Firebird

Neoclassicism

Soon after World War I, Stravinsky's style began to change. He rediscovered the music of 18th-century Europe, and adapted it to create the new, clear-sounding style now known as neoclassicism.

The Soldier's Tale

One of Stravinsky's most popular pieces is *The Soldier's Tale* (1918), a fairy tale for musicians, narrators, and a dancer. This piece of "music theatre" also shows the influence of popular musical forms, such as ragtime.

Performance

Stravinsky was a highly respected conductor as well as composer, famous for his very precise conducting style. He gave numerous concerts, particularly of his own works, and made many recordings of his music. These discs, still available, give us a clear idea of how he intended his music to be played.

Robert Craft

Later in life, Stravinsky took on an assistant, the American musician Robert Craft (b.1923), to help when ill health prevented him from conducting. Together, they also wrote several books about music, and Craft has written about their collaboration.

Stravinsky with Robert Craft

Date on which Stravinsky completed the composition.

Stravinsky's manuscript score of *The Rite of Spring*

Stravinsky used different colours for different instructions.

Manuscript scores

Stravinsky's beautifully hand-written scores show how meticulous he was. He worked very precisely and carefully to achieve just the right effect, giving little room for a performer's or a conductor's own interpretation.

IGOR STRAVINSKY

1882	Born near St. Petersburg, Russia.
1910	*The Firebird* first performed.
1913	*The Rite of Spring* first performed, provoking a riot.
1920	Moves to Paris; neoclassical ballet *Pulchinella* first performed.
1926	Rejoins Orthodox church.
1930	Completes *Symphony of Psalms*
1939	Moves to USA.
1951	Completes the opera *The Rake's Progress*.
1957	Completes *Agon*, ballet score using twelve-tone technique.
1971	Dies in New York.

FIND OUT MORE BALLET DANCE MUSIC OPERA ORCHESTRAS

SUBMARINES

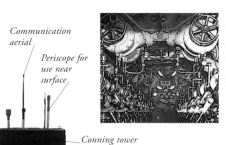

THE ABILITY TO STAY hidden deep under the waves makes the submarine a powerful and effective warship. To travel underwater, a submarine needs a strong hull to resist high water pressure, and engines for both surface and underwater use. Submarines were used effectively as deadly weapons for the first time in World War I. Today, there are two main types of military submarines in operation. A patrol submarine searches for and attacks enemy vessels. A missile submarine carries long-range nuclear missiles.

Anatomy of a submarine

A submarine is encased in a strong steel hull. On top is a conning tower that stands above the water when the submarine is on the surface. Inside the submarine, rooms are arranged on two or three decks. Bulkheads separate the submarine into several sections that can be shut off from each other in case of leaks in the hull.

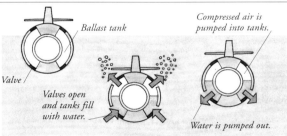

Engines
Submarines have engines that run on nuclear power or on a combination of electric and diesel motors. The engines drive a propeller that pushes the submarine through the water.

Communication aerial

Periscope for use near surface

Conning tower

Hull

Senior officers' mess (living quarters)

Torpedo tube

Bow

Propeller

Stern

Rudder steers the submarine

Hydroplanes tilt to make the submarine dive or rise.

Engine room

Mess for the crew, which can number more than 150.

Wireless office

Galley

Torpedo compartment

Nuclear submarine

Diving and surfacing

On the surface, a submarine floats like a normal ship. To dive, valves let water fill the large ballast tanks on either side of the hull. The extra weight causes the ship to descend. When submerged, the submarine moves up or down using its rudder-like hydroplanes. To surface, the water is blown out of the tanks.

Ballast tank

Compressed air is pumped into tanks.

Valve

Valves open and tanks fill with water.

Water is pumped out.

Submarine floats.

Submarine dives.

Submarine surfaces.

Submersibles

Civil (non-military) submarines are called submersibles. They are smaller than military submarines and are used for carrying out specialized tasks deep underwater, from maintaining ocean pipelines to carrying out salvage operations, or marine research. Submersibles normally dive for only a few hours.

Deepest dives
Most military submarines can dive to depths of about 750 m (2,500 ft). The deepest dive was by a US Navy submarine that achieved a depth of 6.2 km (3.7 miles).

Nuclear submarines
The most powerful submarines are those that carry nuclear missiles, and are driven by nuclear engines. Each missile can destroy a large city, killing thousands of people. Nuclear engines allow a submarine to stay submerged for much longer than other submarines, which have to return to the surface to recharge their batteries.

Torpedoes
Military submarines carry underwater missiles called torpedoes. They are launched from tubes in the submarine's bow or stern. Homing systems, or signals from the submarine, guide modern torpedoes to their targets.

Timeline

1776 David Bushnell's *Turtle* is a waterproof wooden barrel, operated by hand and foot pedals.

1864 The human-powered, iron submarine *Hunley* is the first submarine to sink a ship. Its explosive charge is carried on a long pole.

The Turtle

1901 *Holland VI* is the first submarine with both petrol and electric engines.

1939–45 German submarines (U-boats) hunt Allied shipping in packs, sinking ships with torpedoes.

1954 The first nuclear-powered submarine is the US *Nautilus*.

1986 Crew on the US *Alvin* photographs wreckage of *Titanic*.

2000 The "unsinkable" Russian *Kursk* sinks.

FIND OUT MORE ENGINES AND MOTORS NUCLEAR POWER PRESSURE WARSHIPS WORLD WAR I WORLD WAR II

S

SUMERIANS

IN ABOUT 5000 BC, the Sumerians settled Mesopotamia, the fertile land between the Tigris and Euphrates rivers. They founded farming settlements, which, by 3200 BC, had grown into the world's first cities. As these cities flourished, the Sumerians developed the first known writing system. The Sumerian cities, linked by waterways, developed into a civilization based on a shared language, religious beliefs, art forms, and building styles. The cities traded with each other, but also fought for dominance. In c.2000 BC, eastern desert tribes in search of fertile land moved into the region, and the Sumerian civilization collapsed.

Fertile Crescent

Mediterranean Sea

Uruk

Ur

S

Shrine or temple

Ziggurats were pyramidal structures built with two to seven tiers of mud bricks.

Square bottom tier

The triple staircase at Ur was the first of its kind.

City life

Sumerian cities consisted of mud-brick houses, palaces, and temples enclosed by a large wall. Every day, people left home to farm the surrounding land or fish the rivers. Many worked for the king or the temple. As food production increased, more people were free to work with stone or metal, produce textiles, or make the thousands of mud bricks necessary to build ziggurats and temples.

The city of Ur
This ziggurat dominated the city of Ur, which was dedicated to the moon god Nanna. There were hundreds of gods in the Sumerian religion, and each city had its own special patron.

War
Competition between cities for farmland and materials led to almost endless warfare. The Standard of Ur, a decorated wooden box, shows the ruler leading his soldiers against an enemy. The soldiers are equipped with copper helmets, felt cloaks, spears, and axes.

Gold necklace

Gold helmet

Gold bull on a lyre

Art objects
Sumerian artists were highly skilled. They decorated palace and temple walls with shell and stone inlays. Their craftworkers used imported stone to make statues of humans, animals, and gods. Metalworkers made exquisite jewellery of gold, silver, and rare stones, such as blue lapis lazuli and red cornelian, which they shaped into delicate animals and flowers.

Cuneiform script

The Sumerians invented writing, using a cut reed to draw signs on damp clay. The signs, representing sounds, were combined to form words. The impressions gradually became more cuneiform (wedge-like).

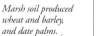

Farming and fishing
Farming communities developed in Mesopotamia between 6000 and 5000 BC. Food was easy to grow in the fertile soil of the marshes. Outside the marshes, the settlers gradually banded together, and built canals to irrigate the land. They cultivated the soil, and kept sheep, cattle, and pigs. Today, the Marsh Arabs of Iraq farm in a similar way to that of their predecessors, the Sumerians.

Marsh soil produced wheat and barley, and date palms.

Sargon
Legend tells how the baby Sargon was left in a basket on the Euphrates, and the goddess Ishtar gave him an empire. In fact, Sargon of Akkad (2000s BC) was the first conqueror of Sumer and most of Mesopotamia, and the first ruler to unify these territories into an empire.

Symbol for day three   *Symbol for a commodity*   *Symbol for 10 units*

Timeline

5000 BC Farmers and fishermen establish settlements in the Fertile Crescent of southern Mesopotamia.

3200 BC Large cities develop, such as Uruk.

3100 BC Sumerians invent writing.

2700 BC Kings, such as the legendary Gilgamesh of Uruk, rule independent cities.

2600 BC Sumerians trade their produce for luxury items, such as metal and precious stones.

c.2350 BC Sargon of Akkad unites Sumerian cities into an empire.

c.2300–2100 BC Sargon's empire fades. Political power shifts from city to city.

c.2100 BC Ur-Nammu of Ur controls the whole of Sumer, helped by his civil service.

Lapis lazuli
Goat statue, Ur

c.2000 BC Amorites from the Syrian desert invade the region, and Sumerian slowly ceases to be spoken. However, people continue to use Sumerian cuneiform script for monumental and religious inscriptions.

FIND OUT MORE   ASSYRIAN EMPIRE   BABYLONIAN EMPIRE   CITIES   FARMING, HISTORY OF   HITTITES   WARFARE   WRITING

SUN AND SOLAR SYSTEM

THE SUN IS A STAR – a huge ball of spinning gas – that is about 5 billion years old. It is important to us because it is the most massive and influential member of the Solar System. Its gravity keeps Earth and eight other planets, more than 60 moons, and millions of comets and asteroids orbiting around it. Together they make up a disc-shaped system which is billions of kilometres across. They share a past and a future dependent on the Sun.

Inside the Sun

The Sun is an incredibly hot sphere of gas that is generating energy. Its core is particularly hot and dense. Here nuclei of hydrogen collide and fuse to form helium. This reaction produces energy which, among other things, lights and heats the Solar System. The energy passes through the radiation and convection zones to the surface (photosphere), then through the Sun's atmosphere (chromosphere) into space.

Life of the Sun
The Sun is a middle-aged star. As it ages, its appearance will change. In about 5 billion years, the hydrogen in its core will have been converted into helium and the outer layers will swell. It will expand to more than 150 times its present size, becoming a red giant. Mercury will be engulfed and life on Earth will cease. Eventually, the outer layers will drift off, and the remains will shrink to become a white dwarf.

Core 15 million°C (27 million°F)

Photosphere 5,500°C (9,900°F)

Chromosphere 50,000°C (90,000°F)

The Sun's face

Earth is 149.6 million km (93 million miles) from the Sun, but still close enough for observers to make out surface features. Energy generated in the core takes millions of years to reach the surface, the photosphere, where some of it breaks through as sunspots, flares, and prominences.

Sunspots
Disturbances in the Sun's magnetic field produce dark, cooler patches – sunspots – in the photosphere. Sunspots follow an 11-year cycle: they first appear at high latitudes and then increase in number, forming nearer and nearer the Equator during the cycle.

Sunspots are purple and black in this false-colour picture.

A solar prominence forms a loop.

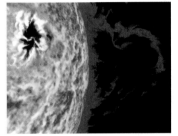

Flares and prominences
An explosive release of energy from the Sun is a flare. A jet of material shoots out from the photosphere, is brilliant for a few minutes, and fades in about an hour. Longer-lived jets are prominences. They may last several months and be 200,000 km (125,000 miles) long. Some shorter-lived prominences form a loop where ejected material is returned to the Sun.

Solar corona
Beyond the photosphere are the chromosphere and the corona – the Sun's inner and outer atmospheres. They are only visible during a solar eclipse when the Sun's face is obscured by the Moon. The corona extends for more than 1 million km (600,000 miles) beyond the photosphere.

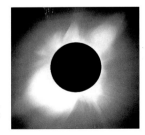

Solar movement

The Sun spins on its axis. Different parts of it take different lengths of time to complete one turn. The equatorial regions move the fastest, taking about 25 days to complete a turn. The polar regions take 35 days.

Ecliptic
The position of the Sun does not alter within the Solar System but it appears to move across Earth's sky. As the Earth spins, the Sun rises at the start and sets at the end of each day. The Sun's path, called the ecliptic, is measured against the more distant background stars. From Earth, the other planets and the Moon are seen to cross the sky close to the ecliptic.

The ecliptic is the Sun's path through the sky.

North Celestial Pole

Celestial equator

Ecliptic

Ecliptic

The Moon and planets cross the sky close to the ecliptic.

South Celestial Pole

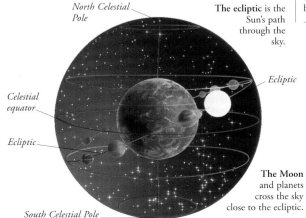

Arthur Eddington
Present knowledge of the nature of stars owes much to an English astronomer, Arthur Eddington (1882–1944). His understanding of the internal structure of stars became the basis of future stellar work. He also produced the first proof for general relativity.

Solar eclipse
When the Moon is directly between the Sun and the Earth, it covers the Sun's face. The Sun is eclipsed. From the part of Earth covered by the umbra (the darker, inner shadow), the Sun appears totally eclipsed. For those people in the penumbra (the outer shadow), the Sun is only partially eclipsed. The eclipse is possible because the Sun and Moon appear to be the same size in the Earth's sky. The Moon is 400 times smaller than the Sun, but it is 400 times closer.

Moon's orbit

Penumbra

Sunlight

Umbra

Earth

Moon

Moon's shadow

The Sun, the nearest star to Earth, is a sphere of gas. About 70 per cent of its mass is hydrogen and 28 per cent helium.

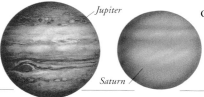

Inner planets

Venus
Mars
Mercury
Earth

Jupiter

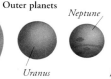

Outer planets

Neptune
Uranus
Pluto
Saturn

The planets
Nine planets orbit the Sun. The four inner ones are made of rock. The four largest, known as the gas planets, consist of large amounts of gas. The most distant, Pluto, is icy rock.

S

Solar System

Almost 99 per cent of the mass of the Solar System is in the Sun. It is not only the most massive but the largest object – 109 Earths could fit across its face; next is Jupiter, 11 Earths across. The smallest objects are tiny specks of dust. Each one of these objects spins on its axis and follows an orbit around the central Sun. The Sun was created about 5 billion years ago, followed by the planets and smaller bodies.

Sun's gravity
The mass of the Sun gives it the most gravitational pull. This keeps the planets and other objects orbiting it. They move fast to prevent being pulled into the Sun. The closest planets orbit the fastest. The more distant planets, where the gravitational pull is weaker, move more slowly.

Biggest planet
Jupiter is the most massive planet. It is made of the most material – 318 times the amount of material that makes Earth. It is also the biggest: it would take 1,330 Earths to fill Jupiter's space.

The axis of Venus is tilted by 178°.

Backward spinner
Each planet spins on its axis as it orbits the Sun. The planets are not upright – their axes are not at right angles to their orbital path. Earth is tipped by 23.5° and spins anti-clockwise as viewed from above the North Pole. Venus, Uranus, and Pluto are tipped over so far they spin on their axes in the opposite direction.

Venus spins backwards, and takes 243 days to turn once.

Pluto's orbit
Neptune's orbit
Uranus's orbit
Saturn's orbit
Jupiter's orbit
Mars's orbit

Neptune

Mercury
Earth
Jupiter
Uranus

Venus
Mars
Saturn

Pluto

Orbits

The planets and asteroids all travel around the Sun in the same direction (anti-clockwise if viewed from above the North Pole) but at different speeds. The orbits are elliptical (oval) and on approximately the same plane. Pluto's is the most inclined, tilted 17°. Comets can orbit the Sun clockwise or anti-clockwise.

Pluto
Pluto has the most elliptical, and longest, orbit.
Venus has the roundest orbit.
Venus

Days and seasons
As Earth spins once every 23 hours 59.6 minutes, any one part of it alternately receives and is hidden from the Sun's light. At the same time, it is orbiting the Sun once every 365.25 days, and different amounts of sunlight are received at different places on its orbit. These differences produce the seasons of a year. They occur because the Earth's axis is tilted by 23.5° as it orbits the Sun. If its axis were at right angles to its orbital path, day and night would always be the same length and there would be no seasons.

The seasons

June: North Pole faces the Sun – longest day in the north and shortest in the south.

March: Northern spring, southern autumn – day and night are equal length.

Sun

Earth's orbit

September: Southern spring, Northern autumn – days and nights are equal length.

December: South Pole faces the Sun – shortest day in the northern hemisphere and longest in the south.

Origins

The Sun and all the objects orbiting it came from the same cloud of gas and dust. The spinning cloud condensed to form the young Sun surrounded by a disc of leftover material. Mercury, Venus, Earth, and Mars formed from the dust nearest the Sun. Farther out, where it was colder, snow and gas joined with dust to form Jupiter, Saturn, Uranus, and Neptune.

Asteroid belt
Smaller bodies in the Solar System, including Pluto and the planetary moons, were formed from material not swept up into the planets. Between Mars and Jupiter is the asteroid belt, made of millions of rocky pieces. The gravity of Jupiter prevented this material from staying together and forming one planetary object.

Johannes Kepler
The first accurate model of the Solar System was produced by the German astronomer Johannes Kepler (1571–1630). He developed three laws to describe the relative distances, speeds, and shapes of the planets' orbits. From then on, it was universally accepted by astronomers that the planets follow elliptical orbits around the Sun.

| FIND OUT MORE | BIG BANG | COMETS AND ASTEROIDS | EARTH | GALAXIES | GALILEO GALILEI | GRAVITY | MOON | PLANETS | ROCKS AND MINERALS | STARS | TIME |

SWEDEN

THE FIFTH LARGEST COUNTRY in Europe, Sweden occupies the eastern half of the Scandinavian peninsula, which it shares with Norway. The Gulf of Bothnia separates most of Sweden from Finland, and the Baltic Sea surrounds the jagged southeastern coastline. About 25 per cent of the country lies in Lapland, in the Arctic Circle. Sweden is a prosperous, environmentally conscious country, boasting one of the world's most efficient welfare systems to support its small population.

SWEDEN FACTS

CAPITAL CITY	Stockholm
AREA	449,964 sq km (173,731 sq miles)
POPULATION	8,800,000
MAIN LANGUAGE	Swedish
MAJOR RELIGION	Christian
CURRENCY	Swedish krona
LIFE EXPECTANCY	80 years
PEOPLE PER DOCTOR	323
GOVERNMENT	Multi-party democracy
ADULT LITERACY	99%

Physical features

About half of Sweden is covered by the Inner Norrland, a region of gentle hills, dense forests of spruce and pine, and more than 100,000 lakes. The bitterly cold, mountainous north includes part of Lapland, shared with Finland, which makes up one-quarter of Sweden's land area.

Sarek National Park
Conservation is a key issue in Sweden, and there is much concern about forest damage from acid rain. Sarek, Europe's first national park, was set up in 1909 and forms part of its largest protected area.

35°C (95°F)   −38°C (−36°F)
16°C (60°F)   −4°C (24°F)
622 mm (25 in)

Climate
Northern winters are bitterly cold, with six months of snow and only a few hours of sunlight. The south has a much milder climate, with only two snowy winter months.

Lakes, rivers, and waterfalls
This peaceful scene epitomizes Arctic Sweden's vast wilderness. Its long rivers rise on the Norwegian border and flow through many lakes to the Baltic Sea, generating hydroelectricity along the way. Sweden's largest lake is Vänern, at 5,584 sq km (2,156 sq miles).

People
Most of Sweden's small population live in the south, enjoying a comfortable lifestyle and equal rights for all. Women constitute half of the work-force, and men share childcare. Swedes have Europe's highest life expectancy because of their good diet and healthcare.

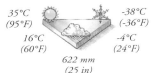

Built-up 2.5%   Forest 70%
Farmland 17.5%
Tundra 4.5%   Barren 5.5%

Land use
Less than nine per cent of the land is available for farming, but small areas of the fertile south are co-operatively used for crops and animals. Sweden is 70 per cent forest, and paper and wood products account for 16 per cent of exports. The country ranks highly in world softwood production.

Swedish family in local costume for midsummer festival, Dalarna

22 per sq km (56 per sq mile)   84% Urban   16% Rural

Volvo car

Farming and industry
Milk, beef, and pork are the main products of the small farming sector. Much larger are the growing technology industries, including Volvo and Ericsson, which have earned Sweden a reputation for design and reliability.

Mutonio
TORNETRÄSK
FINLAND
1
Lule
Kiruna   Torne
2   Lapland
Pite   Gällivare
Arctic Circle   Jokkmokk
Vindel   Uddjaur
3   Luleå
Storsjön   Arvidsjaur   Piteå
Storuman
Ume   Skellefteå
4   Angermann
Umeå
Storsjön   Örnsköldsvik
Ljungan   Östersund   Gulf of Bothnia
5   Härnösand
Sundsvall
Ljusnan
Hudiksvall
6   BALTIC
Mora   SEA
Falun   Gävle
Borlänge   Sandviken
Uppsala
7   Karlstad   Västerås   Norrtälje
Vänern   Örebro   STOCKHOLM
Mariestad   Motala   Huddinge
Uddevalla   Skövde   Nyköping
8   Trollhättan   Vättern   Linköping   Norrköping   Fårö
Borås   Jönköping
Göteborg   Västervik   Visby
Kattegat   Varberg   Oskarshamn   Gotland
9   Halmstad   Växjö   Öland
Helsingborg   Hässleholm   Kalmar
Malmö   Kristianstad   Karlskrona
10   Ystad
A   B   C   D   E

0 km 150
0 miles 150

Stockholm
Sweden's capital is a harbour city, built partly on 14 islands, which are linked by 50 bridges. At the heart is Gamla Stan, the Old Town, founded in 1250. Its narrow, cobbled streets are lined with traditional craft and antique shops. The city also has more than 50 museums.

Central Stockholm

FIND OUT MORE   ARCTIC OCEAN   CARS AND TRUCKS   CONSERVATION   DAMS   DESIGN   ENERGY   EUROPE, HISTORY OF   FORESTS   PAPER   PORTS AND WATERWAYS   SCANDINAVIA, HISTORY OF

SWIFTS AND HUMMINGBIRDS

JET-BLACK SWIFTS AND JEWEL-LIKE hummingbirds belong to the same group of birds. They both have tiny feet and scythe-like wings and are agile fliers. Swifts eat insects, which they catch in mid-air, often twisting and turning after their prey with amazing speed. They hardly ever set foot on the ground, and make their nests in attics and chimneys, or in caves. The main food of hummingbirds is sugary nectar from flowers. They dart from plant to plant, and hover in front of flowers while they drink. Despite being small, hummingbirds are noisy and fearless. They often fight over the best places to feed.

Swifts

There are 92 species of swift, some of which spend most of their life in the air. Swifts often feed, mate, and even sleep on the wing. Many land only to breed. Swifts are found in many parts of the world, but they often migrate to warmer countries in winter when the supply of flying insects dries up.

Flight

Swifts can beat each wing at a different speed. This unusual ability makes them very agile, and they can twist and turn in the air at high speed.

Narrow wings reduce friction at high speed.

Hummingbirds

There are about 300 species of hummingbird, and they are found only in the Americas. Hummingbirds are the most agile fliers in the bird world. As well as flying normally, they can hover in one place, to feed at a flower, and can even fly backwards.

Male

Brilliant metallic colours change as the bird moves.

Feather "boots"

Female

Booted racket-tail

In most hummingbird species, the male is much more striking than the female, but he takes almost no part in raising the young. This male racket-tail has two long tail feathers. They create an impressive display as he tries to attract a mate.

The sword-billed hummingbird's beak is longer than its body.

Hummingbird beaks

The shape of a hummingbird's beak varies according to the flower it feeds at. The sword-billed hummingbird feeds at deep flowers, and its beak is straight. Some hummingbirds have curved beaks, and feed at curved flowers.

This hummingbird is 25 cm (10 in) long, including its beak.

Swift nests

Swifts do not land to collect nesting material. Instead, they make their nests out of saliva and material that they snatch up in the beak or break off with their claws.

Cave swiftlet nests

Chimney swift

This North American swift makes its nest from saliva and tiny twigs. It often glues it to the inside of a tall chimney or ventilation shaft.

How hummingbirds hover

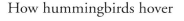

Wings can beat at up to 90 times a second.

Joints inside the wing stay straight.

Wing muscles make up one-third of the hummingbird's weight.

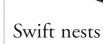

1 The bird sweeps its wings backwards until they touch. This creates a downdraught that pushes the bird upwards.

2 The wings rotate on very flexible shoulder joints as the bird starts to bring them forward again.

3 The forward stroke also creates a downdraught. The moving air again pushes the bird upwards.

4 The wings swing backwards for the next stroke. The movement is usually too fast to be seen.

| FIND OUT MORE | BIRDS | FLIGHT, ANIMAL | FLOWERS | MIGRATION, ANIMAL | NESTS AND BURROWS | SONGBIRDS |

COMMON SWIFT

SCIENTIFIC NAME	*Apus apus*
FAMILY	Apodidae
ORDER	Apodiformes
DISTRIBUTION	Europe and Asia (summer); Africa (winter)
HABITAT	Open air, often above towns and cities
DIET	Flying insects
SIZE	Length, including tail: 18 cm (7 in)
LIFESPAN	About 15–20 years

SWIMMING AND DIVING

SWIMMING IS BOTH a popular recreation and an important competitive sport. It involves using legs and arms against the water to propel the body along. It is an excellent form of exercise, and a good way to learn to swim is to use buoyancy aids, such as water-wings, when practising strokes. Diving, in which a person enters the water head first, is fun too, although at competitive levels it calls for great agility. In competition, divers perfom about 10 dives from a choice of more than 80 dives recognized by the governing body.

Types of stroke

The four competitive strokes are freestyle (invariably front crawl), backstroke, breaststroke, and butterfly.

Knees begin to bend and part slightly.

Arms stretch out in front.

Breaststroke

This is the slowest stroke. Arms and legs move symmetrically underwater, the legs providing most of the thrust. The arms circle from an outstretched position, pulling through the water, around, and under the chin. At the same time, the legs move with a frog-like kick.

Butterfly

Purely a competitive stroke, butterfly was invented when swimmers began to bend the breaststroke rules. The arms move symmetrically from above the water with an explosive pull. The legs kick up and down together.

Preparing for the powerful arm stroke.

Backstroke

Swimmers lie on their backs in backstroke. The stroke requires alternate arm pulls, windmill style, and a flutter kick, in which the legs move up and down in the water.

Gertrude Ederle

First woman to swim the Channel in 1926

Cross-Channel swimming

Of all the long-distance sea swims, the Channel between England and France – 34 km (21 miles) minimum – has always provided the greatest challenge.

Front crawl

This is the fastest stroke, so it is used in freestyle races, but it may also be performed slowly. It is a popular recreational stroke and is used in long-distance swimming. The swimmer lies face down in the water. Both arms and legs move alternately – the arms pull down through the water from an outstretched position, and the legs move up and down.

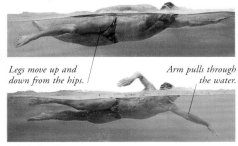

Legs move up and down from the hips.

Arm pulls through the water.

The body rolls from side to side.

Arm comes out near the thigh.

Mark Spitz

American swimmer Mark Spitz (b. 1950) set an an unprecedented record when he won seven gold medals at one Olympic Games. At Munich in 1972, he won the 100- and 200-m freestyle and butterfly, and swam in three winning US relay teams, with world records in all events.

Swimming

Swimming is a major Olympic sport. Before going on to championship meetings, children can compete in their own age groups in swimming galas. Other aquatic sports involving swimming include water polo and synchronized swimming. The former is a seven-a-side ball game; the latter is a kind of underwater ballet.

Racing

Races are started from blocks, and electronic touch-pads at the end of the pool enable major events to be timed to one-thousandth of a second. Olympic-size pools are 50 m (164 ft) long.

Diving

There are two standard diving events – the springboard, 3 m (10 ft) above the water, and the fixed platform, or highboard, 10 m (33 ft) high. The diver performs aerial manoeuvres such as twists and somersaults before entering the water. Points are awarded for technique and style.

Cliff diving

Cliff diving is a popular show for tourists in some Hawaiian and Mexican resorts, such as Acapulco, shown here. Divers plunge 35 m (115 ft) or more into water perhaps only 4 m (13 ft) deep, avoiding projecting rocks as they do so.

Types of dive

There are six main types of dive: forward, backward, twist, inward, reverse, and handstand.

Handstand dive

Handstand, or armstand, dives are performed from the highboard. The diver goes into a steady handstand on the edge of the board before proceeding with the dive.

Backward dive

In the starting position for a backward dive, the diver must keep a straight body, with head up. The arms are swung upward just before take-off from the platform or springboard.

Forward dive

Forward dives may be performed with a run-up as well as from a standing position. As with all dives, the body should enter the water straight, with legs, arms, and hands extended.

FIND OUT MORE

HEALTH AND FITNESS   MEXICO   OLYMPIC GAMES   SAILING AND OTHER WATER SPORTS   SPORT

SWITZERLAND AND AUSTRIA

MOUNTAINOUS AND LAND-LOCKED, Switzerland and Austria sit in the heart of Western Europe, with the tiny principality of Liechtenstein tucked in between them. This central position, and some of Europe's longest rivers, have enabled the three countries to take advantage of trading routes between east and west, and north and south. Switzerland's lack of raw materials has led to the development of specialized high-tech industries, which have made the country rich. Austria's mineral resources supplement its income from farming, and the picturesque lakes and mountains of all three countries attract millions of tourists.

Communications

Treacherous mountain passes were the only routes through the Alps until tunnels and high bridges were engineered. Switzerland's St. Gotthard traffic tunnel is the world's longest road tunnel, and stretches for 16 km (10 miles). Rivers have provided links for centuries. The river port of Basel on the Rhine connects Switzerland to the North Sea, while the mighty Danube joins Austria to the Black Sea.

Train on a high mountain bridge, Switzerland

Physical features

The highest mountains in Europe, the Alps, cover 70 per cent of Switzerland, 75 per cent of Austria, and much of Liechtenstein. Dense coniferous forest dominates Switzerland and is scattered around Austria and Liechtenstein. Two great rivers, the Rhine and the Danube, provide access to the north and south.

Alps

Forming a vast, rocky barrier between northern and southern Europe, the Alps are some of the most impressive mountains in the world. They range across western Europe and are at their most dramatic on the Swiss-Italian border, where the icy Matterhorn rises to 4,478 m (14,691 ft). The Alps are fragile, and tourism is controlled.

Matterhorn

Regional climate

19 (66) -1°C (30°F)

813 mm (32 in)

In Switzerland, Austria, and Liechtenstein, alpine regions are cooler and wetter than the valleys, and have a lot of snow. Switzerland's climate varies, and south-facing mountains are much warmer than northern slopes. On the plateau, summers are warm, and dry winds often bring high winter temperatures. Austria has a high rainfall in the west.

Austrian plains

Broad, fertile plains surrounding the River Danube and its tributaries cover part of northeastern Austria. The small, privately owned farms ensure Austria is self-sufficient in potatoes, sugar beet, and cereals. Surplus crops are exported. Cattle graze on mountain slopes.

Swiss lakes

Switzerland has some of the most scenic and famous lakes on the European continent, including the two largest lakes in Western Europe, Geneva and Constance. Pollution is affecting some of the more popular lakes, such as this tranquil area of Lake Silser, near St. Moritz.

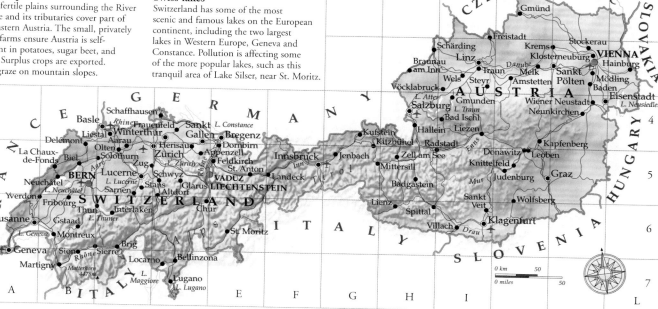

Switzerland

Switzerland is a land of isolated valleys, divided into 26 provinces. A united confederation since 1291, Switzerland has a strong central government. The country has a long history of neutrality in war, and now many international organizations have their headquarters in Geneva. Successful banking and high-tech industries have made Switzerland the world's wealthiest country.

Bern

Home to more than 130,000 people, Switzerland's ancient capital, Bern, dates from the 11th century. Its streets mix historic medieval buildings with modern factories and offices. The bear is a city symbol and its namesake market is a colourful scene.

A panoramic view of Bern

People

Swiss people are the richest in the world, but their costs of living are high. The most multilingual of all European countries, Switzerland has three main languages, with German most used. The Swiss people vote on all major political issues, but two conservative cantons did not grant women the vote until 1989.

Dairy farming
Arable land is scarce in Switzerland, but mountain cattle-grazing has turned the country into a leading exporter of dairy products. Milk from the cows is used to make a wide range of cheese, and chocolate, invented by Henri Nestlé (1814–90).

Industry

About 35 per cent of the labour force work in manufacturing, one of the highest levels in Europe. The Swiss have a world-wide reputation for their precision engineering, especially for making clocks and watches. In 1968, they invented the quartz watch. Other important industries include making optical instruments and the growing chemical and pharmaceutical sector, which employs about ten per cent of the work-force.

Tag Heuer watch

Drug capsules

SWITZERLAND FACTS

CAPITAL CITY Bern

AREA 41,290 sq km (15,942 sq miles)

POPULATION 7,200,000

MAIN LANGUAGES German, French, Italian, Romansch

MAJOR RELIGION Christian

CURRENCY Swiss franc

LIFE EXPECTANCY 79 years

PEOPLE PER DOCTOR 294

GOVERNMENT Multi-party democracy

ADULT LITERACY 99%

Banking
Financial stability, political neutrality, and strict secrecy laws combine to make Switzerland a major banking centre. Foreign investors are attracted by low taxes, and freedom from investigation by tax officials.

Austria

Once the centre of the Austro-Hungarian Empire and a major European power, Austria today is a small, industrialized republic. It has close ties with Switzerland and its powerful northern neighbour, Germany, with which it shares many aspects of language and culture. Nearly 94 per cent of the people are ethnic Austrians.

Vienna

One of the most beautiful cities in Europe, Vienna was once the capital of the Holy Roman Empire. Many of its historic buildings, including St. Stephen's Cathedral, survived the bombs of World War II (1939–45). Others, such as the Opera House, were rebuilt.

St. Stephen's Cathedral

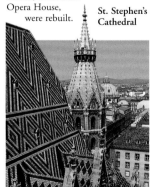

Skiing

Austria's winter sports bring in one-third of the country's tourist income, and more than 10 million people holiday in the Alps every year. Skiers flock to premier alpine resorts, such as St Anton, attracted by heavy snow, breathtaking views, and modern facilities.

Hydroelectric power
With limited fossil fuels, Austria has to rely on its fast mountain streams to provide power for its steel and manufacturing industries. The Danube has also been harnessed to provide 40 per cent of power used.

Music

Many great composers were Austrian, including the Strauss family, who composed the Viennese waltz. Spring's Festival of Vienna hosts concerts, balls, operas, and theatre performances.

AUSTRIA FACTS

CAPITAL CITY Vienna

AREA 83,858 sq km (32,378 sq miles)

POPULATION 8,100,000

MAIN LANGUAGE German

MAJOR RELIGION Christian

CURRENCY Euro

LIFE EXPECTANCY 78 years

PEOPLE PER DOCTOR 333

GOVERNMENT Multi-party democracy

ADULT LITERACY 99%

Liechtenstein

Nestling between the Rhine and the Alps, this tiny principality has close economic ties with Switzerland. A busy financial centre, its economy is highly industrialized. The people of Liechtenstein enjoy a high standard of living and traditional family life.

Lifestyle
Liechtenstein is known for its vineyards, forested nature reserves, and postage stamps. Most people are ethnic Liechtensteiners, but about 35 per cent are Swiss and German. Most disagree with equal rights for women, who only got the vote in 1984.

LIECHTENSTEIN FACTS

CAPITAL CITY Vaduz

AREA 160 sq km (62 sq miles)

POPULATION 32,200

MAIN LANGUAGE German

MAJOR RELIGION Christian

CURRENCY Swiss franc

FIND OUT MORE CHURCHES AND CATHEDRALS   DAMS   EMPIRES   EUROPE, HISTORY OF   EUROPEAN UNION   FARMING   HOLY ROMAN EMPIRE   MONEY   MOUNTAINS AND VALLEYS   MUSIC   WINTER SPORTS

SYRIA AND JORDAN

SYRIA, JORDAN, AND LEBANON together form part of a region called the Middle East that lies between Europe, Africa, and the rest of Asia. The majority of people are Muslim, sharing a common environment and culture. By contrast, the nearby island of Cyprus has strong ties with Europe and its people are mostly Christian. Politics in the region are volatile. The three mainland countries lie on important ancient trade routes, and Syria and Jordan have modern trade links in the form of pipelines that carry oil from countries farther east for shipment to Europe and beyond.

Physical features

The mainland countries of this region are dominated by dry deserts, with strips of fertile land along the Mediterranean coast and in the Jordan Valley. The River Jordan flows 320 km (200 miles) from its source on the border between Syria and Lebanon down to the Dead Sea. Cyprus has fertile plains, mountains, and sandy beaches.

S

Wadi Rum

In southern Jordan, the towering sandstone mountains of the Wadi Rum – an ancient watercourse that is now dry – rise sharply out of the sand to create one of the world's most spectacular desert landscapes. Now a national park, Wadi Rum is home to several Bedouin tribes who live in scattered camps throughout the area.

Troodos Mountains

The Troodos Mountains run for 113 km (70 miles) from east to west in southern Cyprus. The highest peak is Mount Olympus at 1,953 m (6,406 ft). Forests and vines cover the mountains, which contain mineral deposits, including asbestos, gold, and silver.

27°C (80°F)   10°C (50°F)

444 mm (17.5 in)

Regional climate

Summers throughout the whole region are hot and dry and winters cool, with moderate rainfall. Below sea-level, the Jordan Valley has warm winters and scorching summers. In the mountains of Lebanon and Cyprus, winters are colder and wetter with frequent snow.

Bedouins

Nomadic Bedouin peoples and their animals have roamed the deserts of the Middle East for centuries. Living in tents, family groups move around exploiting the limited water and grazing their animals on a seasonal basis. Some Bedouin are camel herders; others keep sheep and goats. Today, their way of life is under threat as governments urge people to settle in towns and cities.

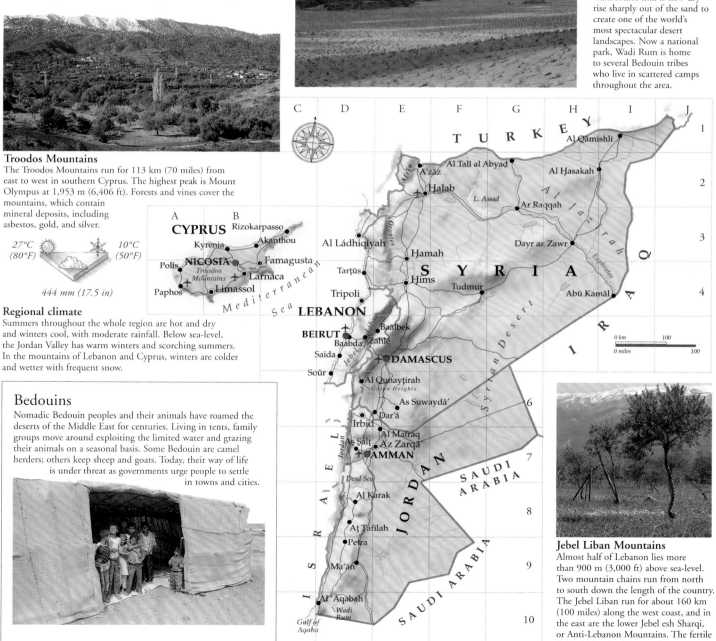

Jebel Liban Mountains

Almost half of Lebanon lies more than 900 m (3,000 ft) above sea-level. Two mountain chains run from north to south down the length of the country. The Jebel Liban run for about 160 km (100 miles) along the west coast, and in the east are the lower Jebel esh Sharqi, or Anti-Lebanon Mountains. The fertile Bekaa Valley lies between the two ranges.

Syria

Inhabited for tens of thousands of years, Syria has a rich cultural history. Only one-third of the land is cultivated and oil is the main source of income. About 20 per cent of Syria is desert, some of which can be grazed. Most Syrians are Muslim Arabs, with a small Kurdish minority who live in the north. The leading political force is the ruling Ba'ath Party.

SYRIA FACTS

CAPITAL CITY Damascus

AREA 184,180 sq km (71,498 sq miles)

POPULATION 16,600,000

MAIN LANGUAGE Arabic

MAJOR RELIGION Muslim

CURRENCY Syrian pound

Sacks of cotton ready for processing

Cotton

Syria's main cash crop is cotton, grown mainly in the north of the country on land watered by the Euphrates and Orontes rivers. Wheat, barley, fruit, and vegetables are also grown. Sheep and goats are raised for meat and milk.

Damascus

Syria's capital, built about 5,000 years ago on the River Barada, is the world's oldest inhabited city. The most important building is the 7th-century Umayyad Mosque, which contains parts of a former Christian church. Nearby, the booths of the Al-Hamidiyah bazaar sell all kinds of craftwork. Small shops sell fresh fruits grown in the orchards outside the city.

Lebanon

This small country on the Mediterranean coast was home to Phoenician traders around 1200 BC. From 1975 until 1991, Lebanon was shattered by civil war between Christians and Muslims. One-third of the land is cultivated, yet farming employs one in five Lebanese workers. The country produces fine wines.

LEBANON FACTS

CAPITAL CITY Beirut

AREA 10,400 sq km (4,015 sq miles)

POPULATION 3,600,000

MAIN LANGUAGE Arabic

MAJOR RELIGIONS Muslim, Christian

CURRENCY Lebanese pound

Beirut

Lebanon's ancient capital, Beirut, lies at the meeting point of three continents. The city is home to more than one million people and is a centre of culture, trade, and tourism. It is now being rebuilt after war damage.

Pickled chillies

Pickled swede

Kibbeh

Pastry

Lebanese food

The national food of Lebanon is *kibbeh,* made of lamb or fish pounded to a fine paste with *burghol* (cracked wheat) and served raw or baked in flat trays or rolled into balls and fried. The Lebanese also love pastries filled with nuts and dates and covered with honey.

Jordan

Apart from a short strip of coast on the Gulf of Aqaba, Jordan is land-locked. Since Eastern Jordan is desert, most people live in the more fertile northwest, close to the River Jordan – the main source of water. At 400 m (1,312 ft) below sea-level, the Dead Sea is the world's lowest point on land. Most Jordanians are Muslim and speak Arabic. Jordan plays a peacekeeping role between Israel and its Arab neighbours.

JORDAN FACTS

CAPITAL CITY Amman

AREA 92,300 sq km (35,637 sq miles)

POPULATION 5,100,000

MAIN LANGUAGE Arabic

MAJOR RELIGION Muslim

CURRENCY Jordanian Dinar

Minaret for calling Muslims to prayer

Mosque overlooking Amman

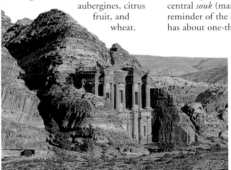

Farming and industry

Jordan receives most of its income from phosphate mining, light industry, and, increasingly, tourism. Although water is in short supply, Jordan grows tomatoes, cucumbers, aubergines, citrus fruit, and wheat.

Amman

Although Amman has been Jordan's capital since only 1921, the city dates back to biblical times when it was built on seven hills. Today, Amman is a mix of old and new buildings, including museums and art galleries. The central *souk* (market) is a lively and colourful reminder of the city's ancient origins. Amman has about one-third of Jordan's population.

Petra

The city of Petra was built 2,000 years ago by Nabatean Arabs who cut tombs, dwellings, and temples into the solid rock. Set in a valley surrounded by red stone cliffs, Petra is reached through the *Siq,* a narrow entrance. Petra is now a great tourist attraction.

Cyprus

Cyprus is the largest island in the eastern Mediterranean. Following Turkish and British rule it became independent in 1959. The majority of Cypriots is Greek- or Turkish-speaking. In 1974, increasing hostilities led to a split between the Greek south and Turkish north.

CYPRUS FACTS

CAPITAL CITY Nicosia (Lefkosia)

AREA 9,250 sq km (3,571 sq miles)

POPULATION 790,000

MAIN LANGUAGES Greek, Turkish

MAJOR RELIGIONS Christian, Muslim

CURRENCY Cyprus pound, Turkish lira

Tourism

Sun, sand, spectacular mountain scenery, and ancient Greek and Roman ruins lure around two million tourists to Cyprus each year. Tourism in the southern part of the island increased greatly in the 1980s.

FIND OUT MORE | ASIA, HISTORY OF | CRUSADES | DESERTS | FARMING | IRAN AND IRAQ | ISLAM | ISLAMIC EMPIRE | MOSQUES | OIL | PHOENICIANS | WARFARE

TECHNOLOGY

THE SCIENCE OF PUTTING inventions and discoveries into practical use is known as technology. A scientist discovers scientific principles, properties, and processes, while engineers use that knowledge to build machines and structures. Technology began in prehistoric times, but did not have a major impact until the 18th and 19th centuries. Then a host of new technologies sprang up, spawning a revolution in industry and at home. Today, it is information technology that is bringing about another major revolution.

Early technology

Prehistoric people pioneered technology when they made the first tools. They smashed pebbles to produce sharp cutting pieces, then later shaped flints into specialist tools such as hand axes, knife blades, and weapons. Tools continued to be made from stone until about 5000 BC, when copper was first smelted and used in the Middle East. In about 3500 BC, metal technology spread with the discovery of bronze. The Bronze Age was then followed by an Iron Age from about 1500 BC.

Stone-Age flint hand axe carefully worked to produce a sharp cutting edge.

Modern technology

The foundations of modern technology were laid in the 1700s, at the beginning of the Industrial Revolution. Inventions transformed traditional craft-based industries into factory-based ones. Key inventions, such as the spinning jenny (1764) and Watt's steam engine (1775), provided the materials, machines, and power necessary for technology to develop.

Quorn is a meat substitute made from mycoprotein – a protein derived from fungi.

Freeze-dried food is light, but still retains nutrients. This type of food is used by astronauts in space.

Tray to hold space foods

Food technology

One of the most important aspects of food technology is preservation. Methods such as salting meat have been practised for thousands of years to stop food spoiling, while canning and refrigeration are more recent. Modern methods include freeze drying, which helps preserve food structure better, and the use of additives. Food technology also includes the manufacture of synthetic substitutes such as TVP (textured vegetable protein).

Materials technology

A range of materials is used for manufacturing goods, machines, and structures. Plastics, for example, are popular because they are cheap and easy to shape. They are used in solid form, as synthetic fibres for textiles, film for packaging, and in composites such as fibreglass. Metals such as iron and aluminium are strong and continue to be important for building machines and structures. Concrete, usually reinforced, or strengthened, is the prime material for building massive structures such as dams, bridges, and skyscrapers.

Reinforced concrete

Information technology

Information technology, or IT, encompasses the revolution in communications and the exchange of information brought about by the widespread use of computers. One aspect of IT is the creation of the Internet, a global network that provides access to "sites" containing a range of information, and allows communication between network "surfers" (users).

Portable, or laptop, computers allow users to work anywhere.

Laptop computer

Engineering

Engineers make technology work. They design and mend machinery and electrical equipment, as well as build a range of structures, mines, and chemical plants. The five main categories of engineering are mechanical, civil, mining, chemical, and electrical engineering.

Civil engineering

Civil engineers are involved in construction engineering projects, which provide a range of structures that are beneficial to the public. These include roads, bridges, dams, tunnels, and skyscrapers. One of the most impressive engineering structures is the 50-km (31-mile) long Channel Tunnel under the English Channel, connecting France with the UK.

Glen Canyon dam, Arizona, USA

Appropriate technology

An appropriate technology can be defined as one which serves local needs, using local resources. Many developing countries cannot afford to develop large projects, so they tend to upgrade and manage existing technologies on a community level. They might make small water turbines to generate power, build irrigation schemes, or produce renewable energy sources, such as wind and solar power.

Irrigation pumps on wheat field

Research biochemist experiments in a sterile environment

Chemical engineering

Chemical engineers build and operate chemical manufacturing plants, such as those used in the petrochemical industry. They develop large-scale processes that research chemists have produced on a small scale in a laboratory. Their approach is to break down the manufacturing operation into a series of steps.

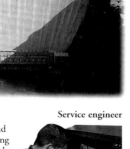

Service engineer

Design and maintenance

A team of engineers is responsible for developing a new product. Design engineers decide how to make it, and what materials to use. Detailed plans are then passed to production engineers who devise its manufacture. After sale, service engineers are on call to carry out maintenance and repairs.

FIND OUT MORE

BRIDGES   BUILDING AND CONSTRUCTION   DAMS   DESIGN   FOOD   INDUSTRIAL REVOLUTION   INFORMATION TECHNOLOGY   INVENTIONS   PLASTICS AND RUBBER

TEETH AND JAWS

BEFORE FOOD CAN BE SWALLOWED, it must be cut up into small pieces so it can travel down the oesophagus and into the stomach. The job of cutting and grinding is carried out by the teeth. These are small, hard structures embedded in the upper and lower jaw bones that grip, bite, slice, and crush food into a paste ready for swallowing. Different types of teeth are adapted to perform particular functions. As a child grows, his or her jaw bones increase in size, until by the end of adolescence they can accommodate a set of 32 adult teeth.

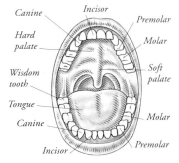

Canine
Hard palate
Wisdom tooth
Tongue
Canine
Incisor
Incisor
Canine
Premolar
Molar
Soft palate
Molar
Premolar

Types of teeth
Each adult jaw contains 16 teeth: four incisors, two canines, four premolars, and six molars. Incisors, at the front of each jaw, are cutting teeth that slide past each other to slice up food. Canines grip and tear food. Premolars and molars have flattened crowns to crush and grind food.

Sharp edge | Sharp edge | Broad crown | Broad crown

Incisor   Canine   Premolar   Molar

Growth of teeth and jaws
We have two sets of teeth during our lifetime. The first set are called primary, or milk, teeth and they gradually appear in babies until a set of 20 is in place. At about the age of six, the roots of some milk teeth loosen and they start to be pushed out and replaced by the permanent or adult teeth.

Milk teeth in gums
Maxilla (upper jaw)
Mandible (lower jaw)

A newborn baby has no visible teeth. Within the upper jaw and lower jaw, however, the milk teeth are developing. These start to erupt at around the age of six months.

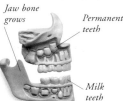

Jaw bone grows
Permanent teeth
Milk teeth

A 5-year-old child has a full set of 20 milk teeth, consisting of four incisors, two canines, and four molars in each jaw. The permanent teeth are developing and will push out.

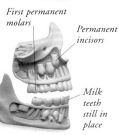

First permanent molars
Permanent incisors
Milk teeth still in place

A 9-year-old child has a combination of permanent and milk teeth. While most of the teeth are milk teeth, the first permanent molars and incisors have already erupted. By age 12, a child's teeth are all permanent teeth.

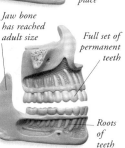

Jaw bone has reached adult size
Full set of permanent teeth
Roots of teeth

A 20-year-old's jaws are fully grown and contain a full set of adult teeth. Some people's wisdom teeth (the molars at the back of the jaw) do not erupt until their twenties. If there is not enough room for them the wisdom teeth are extracted.

Crown is the upper visible part of the tooth.

Gum is soft tissue covering jaw bone.

Blood vessels

Root anchors tooth in jaw bone.

Root canal contains pulp.

Blood capillary supplies tooth with food and oxygen.

Enamel is a very hard material that covers the crown.

Dentine is a living, bone-like material inside the tooth.

Pulp cavity contains pulp.

Cement and peridontal ligament hold root in socket.

Nerve ligament

Jaw bone

Structure of a tooth
Every tooth is made up of three basic layers. Enamel forms a hard cap that protects the tooth. Dentine forms the bulk of the tooth and extends into the root along the root canal. The pulp contains blood vessels and nerves, which allow you to detect pressure when chewing.

Brushing your teeth regularly helps get rid of plaque.

You brush the plaque away from your gums.

Tooth decay
Food leaves behind a sticky residue on your teeth called plaque. Bacteria in plaque release acids that eat away at the enamel. This can expose the inner parts of the tooth, causing tooth decay.

Chewing and biting
The first stage in digestion is chewing, which breaks food up into small particles ready for swallowing. Chewing is controlled by three pairs of muscles that move the lower jaw. The temporalis and masseter muscles pull the lower jaw upwards to crush food. The pterygoid muscles move the lower jaw from side to side, and slide it forwards, to grind food.

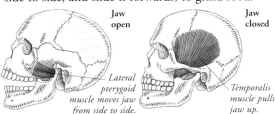

Jaw open

Jaw closed

Lateral pterygoid muscle moves jaw from side to side.

Temporalis muscle pulls jaw up.

Dentistry
In the past, a decaying tooth would have been extracted, but dentists now treat tooth decay by removing affected parts of a tooth, and filling the cavities with hard materials. Artificial crowns can be screwed into a tooth to replace the real thing. Dentists are also concerned with the prevention of tooth and gum disease.

FIND OUT MORE   DIGESTION   FOOD   GROWTH AND DEVELOPMENT   HUMAN BODY   HUMAN EVOLUTION   MEDICINE   MUSCLES AND MOVEMENT   SKELETON   SMELL AND TASTE

TELECOMMUNICATIONS

THE WORLD SEEMS TO BE shrinking thanks to modern telecommunications, which enables us to send messages across the globe in an instant. Telecommunications is the use of technology to send and receive information – such as speech, music, pictures, and documents – over long distances. The devices that make this possible include telephones, radios, satellites, televisions, and computers. The forerunner of modern telecommunications was the telegraph, which sent messages by electrical wires.

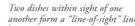

Satellite

Network

Telecommunications devices send information across a network of links that create a pathway between the sender and receiver. The information travels as electrical pulses along copper cables, as flashes of light along optical fibres (thin strands of glass), or as radio or microwave signals between dishes on towers, buildings, and satellites.

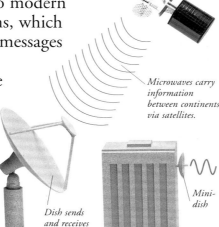

Microwaves carry information between continents via satellites.

Two dishes within sight of one another form a "line-of-sight" link.

Exchange routes signals to correct destination.

Dish sends and receives microwaves to and from satellites.

Mini-dish

Signals are boosted at repeater stations.

Copper cable

Satellite ground station

Fibre-optic cable

Exchange building

Microwave repeater station

Microwave repeater station

Exchange building

Samuel Morse

American Samuel Morse (1791–1872) devised a telegraph system that used a type of modulation called Morse code. Letters and numbers represented by dots and dashes were sent along wires as long and short pulses of electricity.

Messaging technology

Until recently, a fax machine was the best way to send a written message quickly. However, e-mailing from a computer now allows all kinds of information to be sent instantly around the world, including large computer files. Text messaging via mobile phones is another new technology that is rapidly evolving.

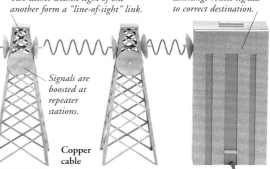

Screen used to read and manage e-mail account

Control panel

Keypad for dialling numbers

Telephone handset

Telephone/e-mail machine

E-mail

E-mail works by sending images and words down a telephone line over the Internet. Most people e-mail from a computer, but e-mail is also becoming available on other devices, including telephone/e-mail machines, such as the one pictured, mobile phones, and even televisions with a digital connection and a keyboard.

Mini keyboard for typing

Modulation

Telecommunications information must be modulated (coded) in some way before it is sent across a network. Radio and television programmes are broadcast by coding the information into a "carrier" radio wave that is sent through the air to a receiving aerial. The aerial sends an electrical signal to a radio or television set, where it is demodulated.

Fax machine

A fax machine sends and receives facsimiles, or copies, of documents and pictures via the telephone line. The machine scans a document and sends the information down the line as electrical signals. The receiving fax machine decodes the signals and prints a copy of the original document.

Keypad for dialling numbers.

A document is sent down an ordinary telephone line.

Telephone handset

Liquid crystal display

Documents to be sent are fed in here.

Heat-sensitive paper prints documents received from other fax machines.

Telephone/fax machine

AM carrier wave

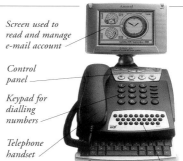

Low amplitude　*High amplitude*

FM carrier wave

Low frequency　*High frequency*

Amplitude modulation

In amplitude modulation (AM), the information is carried by changes in the amplitude, or size, of the carrier wave.

Frequency modulation

In frequency modulation (FM), information is represented by changes in the carrier wave's frequency (the number of waves per second).

Timeline

1793 Frenchman Claude Chappe invents the semaphore, which sends messages using moving arms on towers.

1844 In the USA, Samuel Morse builds the world's first telegraph line.

Early Bell telephone

1876 Scottish-born Alexander Graham Bell invents the telephone.

1878 First telephone exchange opens in New Haven, USA.

1901 Italian inventor Guglielmo Marconi astounds the world by transmitting a radio signal across the Atlantic Ocean, from England to Canada.

1956 Undersea telephone cable installed in Atlantic.

1962 Satellite is first used to make telephone calls.

1977 Optical fibres are used for telephone calls.

1990s E-mail gains mass appeal around the world.

FIND OUT MORE　COMPUTERS　ELECTRICITY　LIGHT　RADIO　SATELLITES　SOUND RECORDING　TELEPHONE　X-RAYS AND THE ELECTROMAGNETIC SPECTRUM

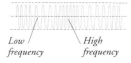

TELEPHONES

"I'LL GIVE YOU A CALL", we often say to our friends, but we rarely wonder how it is that, only a few seconds after entering a number on a keypad, we can be speaking to a friend many kilometres away – even on the other side of the world. A telephone is a device that transforms a person's voice into an electrical signal made up of varying electric currents. This signal travels along copper cables to reach its destination. Sometimes, it is changed into pulses of light and sent along thin glass strands called optical fibres. The signal can also be transmitted as radio waves or microwaves.

Mobile phone

Mobile phones allow the freedom to make calls from almost anywhere because they are not physically connected to the telephone network. They send and receive calls as radio wave signals. Mobile phone technology is fast evolving so that the hand-held devices can now also send text messages, emails and video images, as well as connect to the Internet.

Videophone
Videophones are telephones that allow users to see each other. A tiny camera captures the image of the caller as a signal. The signal is sent to the receiving phone, where it is decoded to display the caller's face. A videophone can be either a mobile phone or a fixed-line telephone.

Aerial inside receives radio waves from mobile phone exchange.

Designs have become more compact over the years.

Mobile phone

Text messaging
Mobile phones allow users to send instant text messages to other mobile phones. Pressing specific combinations of buttons converts the numeric keypad into a text keypad for spelling out words.

Receiving a text message

How telephones work

Once two telephones are linked via the telephone network, the sounds of the speakers' voices are picked up by microphones in the handsets. Loudspeakers reproduce and amplify (boost) these sounds, so that each caller can hear what the other is saying.

Switch hook opens line circuit when handset is down.

Circuit boards contain electronic components.

Keypad
To make a telephone call, the caller picks up the handset, which switches on an electrical circuit. Pressing the keys on the handset sends a sequence of electrical pulses or different tones to an exchange. Each telephone number has a different sequence, so the exchange can easily route the call to the right number.

Keypad

Caller speaks into the mouthpiece.

Earpiece

Earpiece
The earpiece contains a loudspeaker. When the telephone receives an electrical signal from the network, it causes a diaphragm in the loudspeaker to vibrate and recreate the sound of the person's voice at the other end.

Mouthpiece
Inside the mouthpiece is a microphone that contains a thin plastic disk called a diaphragm. The sound of the caller's voice causes the diaphragm to vibrate. As it vibrates, it generates an electrical signal that passes down the telephone line to the receiving telephone.

Handset

Telephone network

Every call reaches its destination via a network of communications links. A local exchange can make connections with any telephone in the caller's area. Long-distance connections are made via national or international exchanges, or even satellites. Cellular exchanges handle the radio signals that carry calls to and from mobile phones.

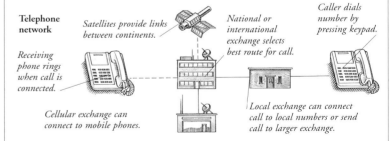

Telephone network

Satellites provide links between continents.

National or international exchange selects best route for call.

Caller dials number by pressing keypad.

Receiving phone rings when call is connected.

Cellular exchange can connect to mobile phones.

Local exchange can connect call to local numbers or send call to larger exchange.

Exchange
An exchange is a building containing equipment that recognizes dialled pulses and tones. It sends calls to the correct destination, represented by a unique telephone number. This process is called switching and is controlled by powerful computers inside the exchange.

Communications satellites
Long-distance telephone calls are often sent as microwave signals via satellites orbiting above the Earth. The satellite strengthens the signal and sends it back to Earth.

Alexander Graham Bell
In 1875, the Scottish-born inventor Alexander Graham Bell (1847–1922) made the first successful transmission of the human voice along an electrical wire. The first words he spoke were to his colleague, Thomas Watson. Bell patented the telephone the following year, beating his American rival Elisha Gray (1835–1901) by just two hours.

FIND OUT MORE   ELECTRICITY   ELECTROMAGNETISM   ELECTRONICS   LIGHT   SOUND   SOUND RECORDING   TELECOMMUNICATIONS   VIDEO

Telephones

Dials

Metal dial, pre-World War I (1914–18)

Coloured plastic dial from the 1930s

Development of the telephone

Speaking and listening cone

Alexander Graham Bell's box telephone, 1876

Dials

Lightweight plastic dial, 1963

Alphanumeric dial, 1960s, with both letters and numbers

Phone engineer's dial, 1960s

Black dial from 1920s Swiss-designed phone

Mobile phones

Hand-portable phone, mid-1980s: like all mobile phones, it contains a built-in radio transmitter and receiver.

Early car phone, mid-1980s

Handset

Picking up the earpiece connected caller to the operator.

Hook for second earpiece if hard of hearing.

Crank handle

Candlestick phone, 1905: users asked the exchange operator to dial the number they wanted to call.

Crank handle telephone, 1890s: user turned the crank to contact the operator in order to make a call, and again to tell the operator that the call was finished.

Mobile phones

Caller speaks in here.

Hinged mouthpiece

Flip-phone, late 1980s: this phone's mouthpiece flips down to reveal the keypad.

Dial

Aerial

Compact mobile phone, mid-1990s

Liquid crystal display

Candlestick phone with dial, 1930s, allowed user to call without going through operator.

Walnut-effect phone, 1920s, moulded in Bakelite plastic to look like wood.

Coloured phone, 1930s: new plastics allowed different coloured phones.

Compact table phone, 1967, designed for use in the home.

Self-contained keypad phone, 1970s: early models had a separate box for the keypad.

Memory keys

Modern phone, mid-1990s: this phone stores frequently called numbers in its electronic memory.

Novelty telephones

Mickey Mouse phone, 1980, based on the popular Walt Disney character.

Trim phone, 1960s, had a luminous dial and electronic ringer.

Bell housing

Separate-bell telephone, 1977: the long cord allowed the caller to move around while talking.

Earpiece

Bells

Transparent phone, 1950s, showed the internal workings of the phone.

Marble phone, 1984

One-piece desk phone, 1970s

Mouthpiece

Leather-bound phone, 1980s

Snoopy phone, 1980, features the character from the cartoon "Peanuts".

TELESCOPES

THE TINIEST OBJECT in the sky can become clearly visible when viewed through a telescope. An optical telescope forms a magnified image of a distant object by altering the path of light rays using lenses and mirrors. There are two main types of telescope. A refracting telescope forms an image by bending, or refracting, light rays using lenses. A reflecting telescope bounces, or reflects, light rays off mirrors so that they form an image. Powerful telescopes allow astronomers to see incredible distances into space. Radio telescopes form images from radio waves emitted by distant stars and galaxies.

Naked eye image   Telescope image

Bringing things closer
Seen with the naked eye, the Moon looks very small, because it is far away. A telescope can magnify (enlarge) this image, making the Moon seem larger and much closer. A telescope's magnifying power is shown by the symbol "x". A telescope with a magnification of 100x, for example, makes objects seem 100 times larger.

Refracting telescope
As light rays from an object enter the telescope, a convex lens (the objective) bends them to form an upside-down image of the object. A second lens (the eyepiece) bends the rays again, magnifying the image.

Chromatic aberration
Light consists of many different colours. When light from an object passes through a lens, each colour bends at a different angle, creating a spectrum of colours around any image that forms. This is called "chromatic aberration". It can be eliminated by adding another lens.

Cutaway of a refracting telescope

Viewing aperture   Eyepiece lens   Laser shows path of rays.   Objective lens

Galileo's telescope
The Italian scientist Galileo Galilei (1564–1642) was the first to use a telescope to systematically study the night sky. He made many important discoveries about the planets and stars.

Sliding tube for focusing   Objective lens

Eyepiece lens   **Galileo's telescope (replica)**

Reflecting telescope
A concave (inward-curving) mirror collects light rays from an object and reflects them on to a flat, angled mirror, which forms an image of the object. A lens (the eyepiece) then magnifies the image for the viewer. Using more than one mirror increases the power of the telescope.

Cutaway of a reflecting telescope

Viewing aperture

Eyepiece lens

Image forms here.

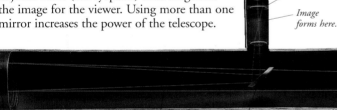

Concave mirror   Reflected light   Flat mirror   Light enters here.

Binoculars
A pair of binoculars consists of two compact refracting telescopes joined together. Each telescope uses two prisms to reflect light rays from the objective lens to the eyepiece lens. The image is focused by adjusting the position of the eyepiece lenses.

Eyepiece lens   Focusing mechanism

Prisms "fold up" the path of the light rays, enabling each telescope to be very compact.

Objective lens

Keck telescope
Many large telescopes are built on mountain tops, where the sky is clear and cloudless. The largest optical telescope, the Keck, is on Mauna Kea volcano in Hawaii. Its collecting mirror consists of 36 hexagonal mirrors, totalling 10 m² (108 ft²).

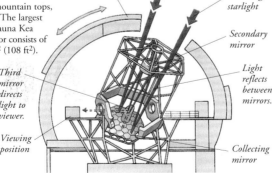

Sliding doors

Incoming starlight

Secondary mirror

Third mirror directs light to viewer.

Light reflects between mirrors.

Viewing position

Collecting mirror

Radio telescope
A radio telescope detects radio waves emitted by stars, galaxies, nebulae, and other astronomical objects. It uses a large dish to focus the waves on to an aerial. The aerial changes the waves into electrical signals, from which a computer generates an image of the object.

Arecibo radio telescope, Puerto Rico

Timeline
10th century The Chinese discover that light rays can be bent by curved pieces of glass.

1608 Dutchman Hans Lippershey invents the telescope.

1673 Englishman Sir Isaac Newton makes a reflecting telescope.

William Herschel's telescope

1789 British astronomer William Herschel designs one of the first large telescopes.

1880 The prism binoculars are invented.

1917 The Mount Wilson telescope is erected in California, USA.

1931 American engineer Karl Jansky discovers that radio waves reach Earth from space.

1937 Grote Reber, an amateur US astronomer, builds the first radio telescope.

1948 The huge Hale reflecting telescope on Mount Palomar, California, USA, is completed.

Hubble Space Telescope

1970 The Very Large Array of radio telescopes is set up in New Mexico, USA.

1990 Launch of the Hubble Space Telescope, an optical telescope orbiting 500 km (310 miles) above the Earth.

2002 Giant telescope with 64 radio dishes planned in Chile.

FIND OUT MORE   ASTRONOMY   GALAXIES   GALILEO GALILEI   LIGHT   MOON   NEWTON, SIR ISAAC   STARS   X-RAYS AND THE ELECTROMAGNETIC SPECTRUM

TELEVISION

TELEVISION WAS ONE OF THE most significant inventions of the 20th century; it completely transformed society. Television (TV) works by converting pictures and sound into signals, and sending them out by transmitters, satellites, or underground cables. Television was first developed in the 1920s; it spread rapidly and by the 1980s, almost every American home had a TV set. By bringing information and entertainment directly into the home, television altered daily life. Today, new advances in television technology, including digital and broadband access, mean that TV can also provide interactive choices such as email, shopping, and information services.

Early television
The first television service began in the UK in 1936. By the 1950s, many families had TV sets, especially in the USA. People who could afford an expensive early receiver wanted to stay at home to be entertained. They were impressed by the up-to-date news coverage and the fact that they could see celebrities in their own homes.

Early TV screens were tiny, and the pictures were black-and-white.

Inside television

Widescreen television

A television receiver (TV set) picks up the signals broadcast by a TV station and turns them into images, using a picture tube (known as a cathode-ray tube). The tube produces a series of black-and-white or colour images in rapid succession, creating the illusion that the picture is moving. The set also contains electronic circuits which enable viewers to tune into the channel of their choice.

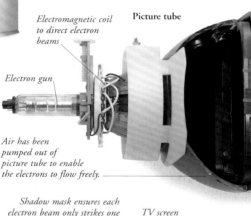

Electromagnetic coil to direct electron beams

Picture tube

Electron gun

Air has been pumped out of picture tube to enable the electrons to flow freely.

Shadow mask ensures each electron beam only strikes one colour of phosphor.

TV screen coated in tiny phosphor dots

Early electron gun

Electron guns
The television screen is just one part of the picture tube. Behind the screen, an electron gun fires three beams of electrons (parts of atoms) at the screen. These beams correspond to the three colours used in television – red, blue, and green. Mixed together, they produce full-colour images.

Electron guns fire streams of electrons towards the screen.

Producing a colour picture
The screen is coated with thousands of tiny dots of phosphor. When the electrons hit these dots, they cause them to glow and produce a red, green, or blue image, depending on the kind of phosphor. The strength of each electron beam varies according to the intensity of colour needed. Because 25 to 30 images are produced on screen every second, TV pictures appear to move.

Vladimir Zworykin
Russian-born scientist Vladimir Kosma Zworykin (1889–1982) did most of his work in the USA. In 1923, he patented the iconoscope television camera tube, the device that made electronic television possible. He followed this with other improvements in television systems.

Uses of television

Television broadcasts cover every area, from drama to documentary. TV informs, educates, and entertains us, depending on what we choose to watch. And, with audiences in the millions, information is spread further than ever before.

Millions watch the soccer World Cup live on TV.

Sponsorship
To raise awareness of their products, some companies sponsor television programmes or advertise during commerical breaks. Many TV programmes and events are underpinned by sponsorship money. Popular sports such as football have gained, with some benefits passed on to sports fans, such as funds for safer stadiums.

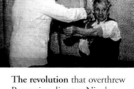

The revolution that overthrew Romanian dictator Nicolae Ceauçescu (1918–89) was shown live on television.

Current affairs
Thanks to television, we can now watch history as it is made, anywhere in the world, and are better informed than ever before. Satellites beam television signals around the world in seconds. Viewers can watch news events as they happen.

Ernie

Bert

Educational television
Television provides educational programmes for children and adults. Programmes are part of correspondance learning up to university level, being accessible to people in remote areas, or to those with limited time.

Sesame Street is an American programme that helps children learn to read.

Making a news programme

Before a programme appears on your screen, it is carefully produced (planned and put together). News programmes are planned only hours before screening. The news team meets to decide which of the day's stories to include; these are researched and a script is prepared. A news broadcast may also include location reports – stories filmed outside the studio.

Light, portable video camera

Houses of Parliament, London, UK

Reporter

On location

Only one person is needed to work a video camera, so a reporter and camera operator can easily produce a simple news report on location. The operator is careful to include an identifiable scene in the background.

Original tape

New tape to be broadcast

Editing equipment

Editing suite

An editor gathers together the camera operator's original video tapes and copies the best sections from each on to another tape in the order in which they will be broadcast. This is done in an editing suite, where video recorders, monitor screens, and vision mixers are linked together with a computer.

In the studio

The live news programme *Newsround* is made for younger viewers by the BBC in the UK, and is broadcast five days a week. As with most programmes, it is made inside a TV studio. The presenter stands in front of a highly graphic, brightly lit set, reading the day's news stories from the autocue.

Autocue

The autocue enables the presenter to see the script while looking directly at the camera. A small computer screen just below the camera lens displays the words and reflects them up on to a diagonally-mounted sheet of glass in front of the camera. Although the news reader can see the words, they are invisible to both camera and viewer.

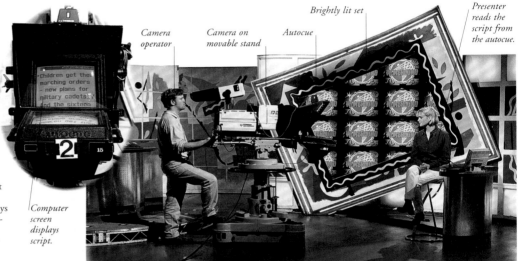

Computer screen displays script.

Camera operator

Camera on movable stand

Autocue

Brightly lit set

Presenter reads the script from the autocue.

The gallery

The gallery (control room) is where the material to make the news broadcast is coordinated during transmission. This includes sequences from the studio cameras, outside broadcasts, music, and graphics. Monitors (video screens) display the different material.

Mixing desk

Different shots are prepared for transmission by a vision mixer, seated at a computerized mixing desk. The vision mixer combines the different elements, fading, jump-cutting, or blending from one sequence to another.

Clock, to check the timing of each part of the programme

Mixing desk, where video, sound, and graphics are mixed together

The rows of buttons on a mixing desk are known as buses and banks.

The team in the studio and gallery talk to each other via microphones.

TV staff

The director and vision mixer sit in the gallery during the live broadcast. The director decides what image should appear on the screen, and for how long. He or she instructs the vision mixer. The producer has overall control.

Timeline

1923 Vladimir Zworykin begins to develop electronic camera tube.

1926 Scottish inventor John Logie Baird (1888–1946) demonstrates his mechanical television system.

1929 Experimental television transmissions begin in England, using Baird's TV system.

1936 World's first regular TV broadcasts begin in England, using electronic system.

1951 First colour broadcasts in US.

1960 Japanese firm Sony introduces all-transistor TV receivers.

1962 Telstar satellite relays television signals across the Atlantic.

1979 Flat-screen pocket television.

1990s Digital and broadband TV.

FIND OUT MORE   ADVERTISING AND MARKETING   CARTOONS AND ANIMATION   DRAMA   ELECTRONICS   INFORMATION TECHNOLOGY   INVENTIONS   RADIO   TELECOMMUNICATIONS

TENNIS AND OTHER RACKET SPORTS

LAWN TENNIS is the most popular and widely played of the racket sports – those in which rackets are used to strike balls of various shapes and sizes across a net or against a wall. Other racket sports are: squash, played in a walled court; badminton, played across a high net; and table tennis, played on a table. Real tennis is an ancient game still played in a few places, and the relatively new sport of racquetball is popular in some parts of the United States.

Server stands sideways on to the net with feet slightly apart.

Racket arm is bent behind the neck as the ball is thrown up.

Eyes on the ball

Racket arm is fully outstretched when hitting the ball.

Server puts power into the serve, using the leg muscles

Serving the ball to start a point

T

Lawn tennis

In tennis, players hit a ball over a net into the opponent's court so that it cannot be returned. When they win a point they score 15, then 30, 40, and game. A player with six games, two ahead of the opponent, wins a set. Tennis is played as singles with two opponents, or doubles, with opposing pairs.

Real tennis
Real, or royal, tennis was played by French and English royalty in the Middle Ages. The few courts around the world are bounded by open windows and doors and sloping roofs.

Tennis racket and balls

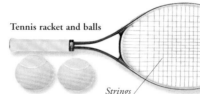

Strings

Tennis balls
White or yellow, tennis balls are 6.5 cm (2.5 in) across. They weigh about 57 g (2 oz) and must conform to a specific standard. In major tournaments, the balls are changed every nine games.

Tennis racket
The frame of a racket is made of wood, metal, or other material, such as carbon graphite, and must be evenly strung. The racket must be no longer than 81.3 cm (32 in) or wider than 31.75 cm (12.5 in) .

Tennis court

Tennis court
Tennis is played on a court 23.77 m (78 ft) long. It is 10.97 m (36 ft) wide for doubles, and 8.23 m (27 ft) wide for singles.

Andre Agassi

US tennis star Andre Agassi (b.1970) is one of the few players to have won six Grand Slam titles in his career. He also won an Olympic gold medal in 1996. The player has a reputation as a rebel on court due to his loud dress sense.

Squash

Mainly a singles game, squash is played in an enclosed court with four walls. The players use the same floor space. The object is to hit the ball against one or more walls, provided one is the front wall, so that the opponent cannot return it before it has bounced twice on the floor.

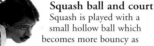

Taking a low ball

Squash ball and court
Squash is played with a small hollow ball which becomes more bouncy as the air inside gets warm and expands. The ball must land below the out-of-court line marked all around the court, and must not hit the board at the base of the front wall.

Squash court

Racquetball racket and ball

Racquetball
This game was invented in 1950 in the USA, where it has overtaken squash in popularity. The ceiling is used as well as the walls. As in squash, the ball must always hit the front wall and may bounce only once on the floor.

Badminton

The aim of this game is to hit a feathered shuttlecock over a high net into the opponent's court. The shuttle must be returned before it touches the ground. Matches are usually the best of three games, with a game being won by the first player to reach 11 or 15 points, two ahead of the opponent.

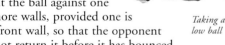

Badminton racket

Shuttlecocks

Badminton equipment
Shuttlecocks may be plastic, but most players prefer to play with shuttles made of a "skirt" of goose feathers fixed in a cork base. Rackets, made mostly of metal or carbon fibre, are extremely light.

Badminton court

Table tennis

Players aim to hit a ball over a net so that the opponent cannot return it. The ball must bounce before being hit. For service, it must bounce on the server's side first. The first player to score 21 points, wins.

Ball

Bat

Table

Table tennis
The small ball is made of light plastic. The blade of the wooden bat may be covered in pimpled rubber on both sides. The net is 15.25 cm (6 in) high. The table measures 2.74 x 1.52 m (9 x 5 ft) and is 76 cm (30 in) high.

FIND OUT
MORE

BALL GAMES

HEALTH AND FITNESS

MEDIEVAL EUROPE

OLYMPIC GAMES

SPORT

T

TEXTILES AND WEAVING

A TEXTILE IS ANY MATERIAL that has been made from fibres, linked together. For thousands of years, all textiles were made from natural fibres, obtained from either animal or plant sources. From the 20th century, chemical processes have produced synthetic (artificial) fibres as well. Most textiles are made by weaving (textile comes from the Latin *texere*, meaning to weave), but they can also be made by knitting, or binding together in various ways. Finished textiles are made into a huge variety of goods, including clothing, furnishings such as curtains and carpets, string, rope, and parachutes.

Jacket, made from oil: mixture of nylon and Pertex® artificial fibres, designed to keep the wearer dry and not too hot.

Nylon rucksack: durable and waterproof

T-shirt: a mix of natural cotton and synthetic polyester fibres; polyester helps the t-shirt keep its shape.

Wool
Wool comes from the fleece of sheep, goats, camels, and llamas. It is popular for making clothes, carpets, and upholstery, as it is warm, strong, stretches, and is absorbent.

Undyed fleece

Main wool producers are Australia, New Zealand, South Africa, and Argentina.

Spun wool

Fibres
Natural fibres include wool and silk from animals, and cotton, flax, and hemp from plants. Synthetic fibres, such as polyesters and acrylics, are made from wood, coal, or oil. Each fibre has different qualities; manufacturers may combine two or three kinds, to produce an "ideal" fabric.

Woven rug

Denim, a tough fabric, is made from woven cotton.

Waterproofed textiles, such as those used in these trainers, have been coated with a thin layer of resin.

Spinneret and cooling nylon filaments

Crude oil

Nylon
Nylon, a synthetic fibre, is made from chemicals found in crude oil. When the chemicals are heated, they form a liquid, which is forced through a spinneret and cooled to form filaments. These are then spun into a yarn.

Making yarn
Before a fibre is made into cloth, it must be spun into yarn (thread). Most natural fibres are very short and must be spun into longer, stronger yarn. Artificial fibres are produced as a continous thread and are spun to make them stronger, rather than longer, or are spun to combine them with natural fibres.

Spinning cotton
Cotton can be spun by hand or by vast factory machines. The machines first squeeze the cleaned fibres together between rollers, into a mat. This is then divided and twisted together into finer and finer threads.

A cotton boll (a clump of fibres) may comprise 500,000 short, white fibres.

Spinning cotton by hand in India

Weaving
Once produced, yarn can be made into cloth. One of the most common means of making cloth is weaving. This is an ancient craft; the earliest evidence of weaving dates from 5000 BC. Most weaving is carried out on a frame called a loom; these can be either massive, machine-powered factory looms, or hand looms.

Weaving a rug by hand

Warp threads must be very strong.

Shuttle

Hand loom

Mechanized looms in a textile factory

The loom
A set of parallel threads, called the warp, are stretched lengthways on the loom. The threads that run widthways are called the weft. The weft is carried over and under the warp by a device called a shuttle. This process interlaces the weft and warp to make fabric.

Textile industry
Until the 18th century, weaving was a craft practised in the home on a small scale. The advances in technology made during the Industrial Revolution massively increased the amount a weaver could produce. Mechanical looms now produce thousands of metres of fabric in a day.

FIND OUT MORE AUSTRALIA CHEMISTRY CLOTHES AND FASHION DYES AND PAINTS FARMING FURNITURE INDUSTRIAL REVOLUTION OIL SHEEP AND GOATS TRADE AND INDUSTRY

THAILAND AND BURMA

LYING SIDE BY SIDE in the west of mainland Southeast Asia, Thailand and Burma (also known as Myanmar) resemble each other in many ways. Both countries have mountains and forests in the north, fertile river valleys, similar mineral resources, and a shared religion – Buddhism. However, their governments and economies differ greatly. Thailand is a wealthy, democratic monarchy; Burma is isolated and undeveloped, with a poor human rights record.

Physical features

The densely forested mountains in the north of Thailand and Burma give rise to many rivers, such as the Chao Phraya and the Irrawaddy, that cut through the fertile countryside on their way to the coast. The western coast on the Andaman Sea is dotted with many islands.

River Irrawaddy
The Irrawaddy is Burma's largest river. It rises in the north, and flows for 2,090 km (1,300 miles) to a huge delta on the Bay of Bengal. Rivers provide the Thai and Burmese people with water to irrigate the rice paddies and a cheap, efficient means of transport.

Monsoon rainforest
The border between Burma and Thailand is covered in thick, impenetrable monsoon rainforest. In the 1980s, the destruction of large areas of forest to provide timber, especially teak, for export led to serious flooding. As a result, in 1989, the Thai government banned logging.

Andaman Sea
To the west of the narrow strip of Burmese land at the top of the Malay Peninsula lies the Andaman Sea, which is part of the Indian Ocean. It is bordered by mangrove swamps, which help to prevent coastline erosion. Dotted with hundreds of tiny, remote islands, this area is a growing tourist attraction.

Regional climate
Thailand and Burma have a monsoon climate with three seasons: rainy from May to September, mild and dry from October to February, and hot in March and April. In the south, rainfall is spread over the whole year. The average temperatures are high.

27°C (80°F)   25°C (77°F)

2,008 mm (79 in)

Hill tribes
The mountainous and largely forested region where Thailand, Burma, and Laos meet is known as the Golden Triangle. Here, poor hill tribes live in villages, farming small plots of land, that have been cleared of trees using the "slash-and-burn" technique. They also cultivate opium poppies, which are used to make heroin and other drugs for the illegal drug trade.

Akha tribeswoman with opium pipe

Thailand

Bordered by Burma, Laos, Cambodia, and Malaysia, the kingdom of Thailand, once called Siam, was established in the 13th century, and the country has remained independent for much of its history. It was the only country in mainland Southeast Asia never to be colonized. Its name in the Thai language is Muang Thai, meaning "land of the free". Modern Thailand has one of the world's fastest growing economies, although there is still great poverty in rural areas, where 80 per cent of the people live. Bangkok, the capital and only big city, is very overcrowded.

Ethnic Thais
Most Thais are descended from people who began migrating south from China nearly 2,000 years ago. As a nation, they are traditional Buddhists. About 12 per cent of the population are ethnic Chinese.

King of Thailand
Thailand's ninth king, Bhumibol Adulyadej, came to the throne in 1946. His family, the Chakris, have ruled Thailand since 1782. The king has immense personal prestige and criticism of him is frowned upon.

Rice
About a quarter of Thailand is used for farming, mostly for growing rice in the fertile river valleys. Every year, 19,440,000 tonnes (21,488906 tons) are produced. Rice is the basis of all main meals, usually accompanied by at least five other dishes, flavoured with fish sauce and coriander.

Industry
Although only 15 per cent of Thai workers are employed in industry, manufacturing is increasingly important. In recent years, American and Japanese companies have set up factories in Thailand, which is now a leading producer of electronic goods. Other manufactures include rubber and jute products. Thai mines produce tin, other metals, and precious stones.

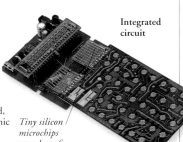

Integrated circuit

Tiny silicon microchips store lots of information.

Crops
More than half of Thailand's workers are employed in farming. Important crops include cassava, which is the source of tapioca, sugar-cane, and pineapples. Thailand is the world's biggest exporter of canned pineapple, and a leading producer of natural rubber. Thais also grow bananas, coconuts, jute, and cotton.

Pineapple

Cassava

Tourism
Thailand's ornate Buddhist temples and cultural heritage draw thousands of tourists every year. New golf courses are being built to attract Japanese visitors, and the northern hill villages, island resorts, and unspoilt beaches are also popular with holidaymakers.

Sugar-cane

Bangkok
Thailand's capital was originally built on a network of canals many of which are still used for transporting goods. For a city of over six million people, Bangkok has relatively few major roads and limited public transport, giving it the world's worst traffic jams. Many commuters equip their cars as offices, with phone and fax, so they can work on the move.

Floating market on a Bangkok canal

Burma

When Burma became independent in 1948, it adopted a policy of political and economic isolation that reduced this once wealthy nation to one of the poorest on Earth. Revolts by hill peoples, and a military government have kept out foreign influences.

Teak logging
In 1990, Burma had about 70 per cent of the total world reserves of teak. Selective logging of teak using elephants is now seldom practised, and today vast areas are cleared by machine. Deforestation has caused erosion, and replanting is rare.

Rubies
The rubies mined in the northeast of Burma are considered to be the world's finest, prized for their glowing, deep red colour. Burma is also rich in silver, copper, jade, lead, zinc, and tin, and has extensive reserves of natural gas and oil.

Fishing
Fish served with vegetables form an important part of the Burmese diet. Shrimps and saltwater fish are caught off the coast. To harvest the freshwater fish that abound in the rivers, people build fishing huts on stilts over the water.

FIND OUT MORE

ASIA, HISTORY OF · BUDDHISM · CONSERVATION · CRYSTALS AND GEMS · GOVERNMENTS AND POLITICS · RAINFOREST WILDLIFE · ROCKS AND MINERALS · TRADE AND INDUSTRY · WINDS

THEATRES

THROUGHOUT THE AGES, theatres have provided two essentials: somewhere for performers to act, and a place for an audience to watch them. A theatre may be a purpose-built environment, such as the Paris Opera House, or it may be as simple as an open-air stage. Either way, theatres provide the setting for performances of all kinds, from plays to opera, and from puppet shows to dance. Most modern theatres have a huge pool of workers including craft workers, prop-makers, set designers, scene painters, make-up artists, and costumiers, as well as the actors themselves.

Roman amphitheatre

History of theatres

The earliest surviving theatres were ancient Greek open-air amphitheatres, in which audiences sat in a semicircle around a pillared stage. The Romans copied the Greek design, but from then until the Renaissance, theatres tended to be a temporary wooden stage.

The rich sat in the galleries; the poor stood in the courtyard.

Theatres through the ages

During the Renaisssance, theatres were once again permanent structures, but with simple interiors. The playwright Shakespeare's theatre, the Globe in London, had three enclosed galleries, but retained an open-air courtyard.

Modern theatres

During the 19th century, theatres became very ornate, but they simplified in design during the 20th century. Today, theatres, such as the National in London, are often housed in complexes, which also contain venues, such as cinemas.

Globe Theatre, UK

National Theatre, UK

Features

In the 1800s, drama became more realistic, with elaborate scene changes. Theatre structure reflected its functions. There were four main features in every theatre: stage, backstage, front of house, and auditorium.

Lighting grid

Central dome is supported by iron girders.

Auditorium has five tiers and seats 2,000 people.

Stage and orchestra pit

The Paris Opera House (built 1862–75) covers 1.2 hectares (3 acres) and was designed by Charles Garnier. The stage is 53 m (175 ft) wide and 26 m (85 ft) deep. It slopes upwards towards the back to let the audience see the action more clearly. The orchestra pit, where the musicians play, is located beneath the front of the stage.

Grand foyer features a mosaic ceiling.

Backstage area contains the "green room" where performers wait for their cue.

Garnier Opera House, Paris, France

Fly tower, with pulley system, hoists heavy pieces of scenery.

Below-stage scenery store

Stage at the Paris Opera House can hold up to 400 people.

Grand staircase

Front of house

The audience enters through an area known as front of house. This provides a space for people to meet before going into the performance, and also houses the box office where tickets are sold. The front of house of the Paris Opera House is one of the world's grandest. It includes a staircase (usual in theatres because seating is on different levels) and balconies, where 19th-century society's opera-goers could be seen arriving, as was the fashion.

Grand staircase, Paris Opera House, France

Auditorium

The auditorium, such as that at London's Theatre Royal Haymarket, contains seating on different levels: stalls, tiered "circles" of seats, and private boxes. The stalls have the best view of the stage; they and the private boxes contain the most expensive seats. The dress circle above the stalls, and the upper circle above that, have cheaper seats. The upper circle (sometimes known as "the gods") has the poorest view.

Theatre Royal, Haymarket, London, UK

Production

Many people are involved in the production of a play – director, actors, designers, make-up, stage managers, lighting, and sound engineers. Rehearsals (meetings held to work out the production) may run over weeks, and end in a full dress rehearsal before the play is performed.

Bill Alexander, theatre director

Director

The director interprets the play and "directs" the action. He or she works with the actors to decide how they should play the characters and speak the lines. The actors read through the script and learn the words. They write notes on their copies, concerning movements, cues, and props.

Props

Articles used on stage, which are not costume or scenery, are known as properties, or "props." Props may be varied, and are the responsibility of the stage manager, who looks after them between performances and makes sure they are left out – often on tables – backstage, where the performers can find them quickly when they are needed.

Audiences cannot see wear and tear.

Papier-mâché crown

Original 1920s' telephone

Simple fastening

Plastic jam

Iron ball and chain

Jam dish

Make-up

Under bright theatre lights, unmade-up faces look pale and flat. Make-up is, therefore, an essential part of theatre. It defines the performers' facial features, and brings characters to life.

Transformation

Theatrical make-up can be used to change the appearance of a face, for example, making actors look older than they really are. Another use of make-up is to produce an obviously unrealistic effect, such as the white face traditionally worn by clowns.

Black and white make-up and red-rimmed eyes give the actor a haggard look.

A stick-on grey beard immediately makes the actor appear older.

Final touches ensure that the make-up stays on under the hot lights.

Lighting

Direct lighting creates dramatic shadows and builds atmosphere; spotlights pick out individuals. Multiple lighting produces a "natural" effect and allows parts of the stage to be dimmed or lit more brightly if necessary. There are special technical rehearsals for lighting.

Spotlight highlights individual performers.

Bank of lights

Production of *Jesus Christ, Superstar*

Kabuki

Kabuki is a traditional theatrical form in Japan. In Kabuki, the all-male cast wears make-up according to 17th-century rules, which have remained virtually unchanged. Each character has mask-like make-up, which identifies them to the audience.

Uzaemo Ichimura, kabuki actor

Orson Welles

The American actor, director, and filmmaker Orson Welles (1915–85) is best known for his classic film *Citizen Kane* (1941). However, his theatre career established him as the leading director of his day. One of his first productions was a version of *Macbeth* (1936), which used an entirely black cast – the first time ever this was done.

Ruff, a 16th-century fashion

Velvet hat

Hat with feathers

Bright colours

Braiding

Leather shoes

Elizabethan man's costume

Original handmade shoes

1940s' woman's costume

Costumes and sets

Most theatre productions need historical costumes and stage sets. Theatres usually employ a person in wardrobe. He or she takes care of the costumes and helps the performers change between acts.

Stage model, *Dream King*

Set designers

Set designers design and create the stage set. First they construct a model. When this is approved, they work with scene painters and carpenters to make the set.

FIND OUT MORE

DRAMA ELIZABETH I FILMS AND FILM-MAKING GREECE, ANCIENT JAPAN, HISTORY OF OPERA RENAISSANCE ROMAN EMPIRE SHAKESPEARE, WILLIAM

TIME

TIME IS LIKE A flowing river, carrying us steadily from the past, which we know, towards the future, which we cannot know. Although we are unable to control time, we can record its passing using measuring devices such as clocks and watches, and calendars that help us to organize and plan our lives. However, time is not constant, and in certain situations it can even slow down. Some scientists think that time may even come to a stop inside black holes in deepest space.

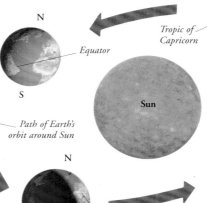

Day
One full day is the time it takes for the Earth to spin once on its axis. Each day contains 24 hours, each hour is made up of 60 minutes, and each minute contains 60 seconds.

Equator

Path of Earth's orbit around Sun

Northern hemisphere

Southern hemisphere

Tropic of Capricorn

Tropic of Cancer

Earth's axis

Sun

Year
A year is 365 days long. This is based on the time it takes for the Earth to orbit the Sun, which is 365 $1/4$ days. The $1/4$ day is impractical, so every four years – except 2000 and other century years – the $1/4$ days are added together to make up one extra day, giving a "leap" year of 366 days.

Seasons
The phases of weather we call seasons are caused by the fact that the Earth's axis is not at right angles to the Sun, but tilts at an angle of 23.5°. This means that, as the Earth travels around the Sun, each hemisphere leans first towards the Sun, giving longer, warmer days, and then away from it, giving shorter, colder days.

Time in modern physics

Scientists had to revise their ideas about the nature of time when the German physicist Albert Einstein (1879–1955) published his theories of relativity. The theories showed that time slows down for objects travelling close to the speed of light. Research has shown that this is true even for slower-moving objects: astronauts who spend a year in orbit age by one-hundredth of a second less than people on Earth.

Astronauts in space

Time on Earth

The passage of time on Earth is measured in terms of the motion of the Earth and the Moon. The rotating Earth turns us towards the Sun, giving day, and then away from the Sun, giving night. Day and night are of equal length during the equinoxes – the two occasions in the year when the Sun is directly overhead at the equator. At the two solstices, when the Sun is directly overhead at one of the tropics, one hemisphere has its longest day, while the other has its longest night.

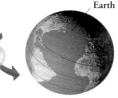

Moon

Earth

Months
There are 12 months in a year. Months last between 28 and 31 days. They were originally based on the time it takes for the Moon to go through all its phases as it orbits the Earth, which is 29½ days

Glass shatters into tiny fragments.

Time's arrow
How can we be sure that time does not go backwards? The proof lies in the increasing disorder of the Universe. For example, when a glass smashes, its orderly arrangement breaks into disordered fragments. Broken glass never reassembles itself, proving that time can move only forwards, from the present to the future.

Each year is named after an animal.

Calendars
The Western world uses the 365-day Gregorian calendar. This is based on the Earth's orbit of the Sun, so the Sun appears in the same place in the sky on the same date each year. Many other calendars have been devised throughout history. The traditional Hindu, Chinese, Muslim, and Jewish calendars are based on the Moon's cycles. The Chinese calendar has 12 months and is 354 days long. The ancient Aztec calendar was solar, like the Gregorian calendar, but consisted of 18 months of 20 days, and five extra days that were considered unlucky.

Chinese calendar

Aztec calendar

At the centre of the calendar is the Aztec Sun god.

Time and speed

To understand how fast an object moves, we need to know how far it travels and how long it takes to travel that distance. The graph below shows the relationship between distance and time for a car journey: the steeper the graph's slope, the faster the car is moving.

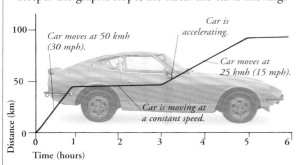

Car moves at 50 kmh (30 mph).

Car is accelerating.

Car moves at 25 kmh (15 mph).

Car is moving at a constant speed.

Distance (km)

Time (hours)

Time zones

To make it easier to set clocks, the world is divided into 24 regions called time zones, each of which is about 15° of longitude wide. These time zones ensure that wherever you are in the world, when the Sun is directly overhead it will be 12 noon. The map shows what time it is around the world when it is 12 noon at Greenwich, England.

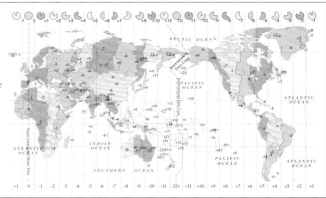

Early time measurement

To tell the time, ancient peoples used the changing shadows cast by the Sun as it moved across the sky during the day, and the movement of stars at night. Later, time-keeping devices, such as sundials, sand clocks, clock candles, and star dials, were developed. The invention of mechanical clocks made these methods redundant.

Sundials
As the day progressed, a shadow cast by the Sun moved slowly around a dial marked with hours.

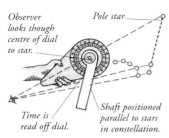

Observer looks though centre of dial to star.

Pole star

Shaft positioned parallel to stars in constellation.

Time is read off dial.

Clock candle
A candle ringed with notches recorded the passing of the hours as it burned down.

Star dial
A device called a star dial was used to find the time from the position of familiar stars and constellations in the night sky.

Sand clock
Sand flowed from the top of the glass to the bottom in a fixed amount of time.

Quartz watch

Most modern clocks and watches are controlled by a thin slice of quartz crystal. Electricity supplied by a small battery makes the crystal vibrate and give out pulses of current at a precise rate, or frequency. A microchip then reduces this rate to one pulse per second. This control signal goes to an electric motor that turns the hands or changes the numbers on the digital display. Most quartz clocks and watches are accurate to within about 15 seconds per year.

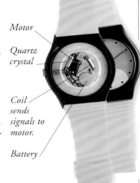

Motor

Quartz crystal

Coil sends signals to motor.

Battery

Quartz watch

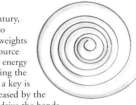

Clock weighs about 30 kg (66 lb).

Caesium clock

Atomic clock
The most accurate of all clocks are atomic clocks, which will lose or gain just one second every 300,000 years. Atomic clocks measure time by recording the natural vibrations of atoms, usually of the element caesium. The second – the basic scientific unit of time – is defined as the time it takes for a caesium atom to vibrate 9,192,770 times.

Mechanical clocks and watches

Early all-mechanical clocks were made in European monasteries and cathedrals in the 13th century. They were powered by falling weights linked to a mechanism called an escapement. Clocks became more accurate when pendulums were used to regulate the escapement. The invention of the mainspring made smaller clocks possible and led to the development of the watch. Early watches were worn around the neck on a chain. Later designs were small enough to fit into a pocket or be worn around the wrist on a strap.

Anchor

Escape wheel

Pendulum

Weight

Escapement
Many pendulum clocks are driven by a falling weight linked to an escape wheel. As the pendulum swings, it rocks a lever called the anchor, causing it to grip and release the escape wheel with a regular motion. One tooth of the wheel escapes with each swing, moving the clock's hands on a little.

Each to-and-fro swing is called a period.

Hour hand

Hours in Roman numerals

Minute hand

Clock face
There are 12 hours marked on a clock face. This means that the hour hand moves around the clock face twice each day. The minute hand revolves once every hour. Many clocks also have a second hand that circles the clock face once every minute.

Falling weight drives the clock mechanism.

This weight acts as a counter-balance.

Pendulum
A pendulum is a weight that swings back and forth on a fixed string, rod, or wire. Each back-and-forth movement takes the same amount of time, and it is this regular motion that makes it useful for time-keeping. In a clock, a pendulum controls the escapement.

Mainspring
In the 16th century, springs began to replace falling weights as the energy source for clocks. The energy stored by winding the spring up with a key is then slowly released by the escapement to drive the hands.

Twenty-four-hour clock
Transport timetables give arrival and departure times using the twenty-four-hour clock. In this system, midnight is 0000 and noon is 1200. Times after noon are given as numbers greater than 1200. For example, 4:00 pm is 1600.

Christiaan Huygens

Dutch physicist Christiaan Huygens (1629–95) built the first practical pendulum clock in 1657, and also found the mathematical rule that links the duration of a pendulum's swing to its length: the longer the pendulum, the longer its swing. Huygens gave an accurate description of Saturn's rings and was first to suggest that light travels as waves.

Timeline
c.2600 BC The Chinese develop a primitive form of sundial.

c.1400 BC The Egyptians use water clocks, which measure time by the flow of water through a vessel with a hole in it.

Chinese water clock

c.890 Clock candles appear in England.

c.1300 Mechanical clocks are built in Italian and English monasteries.

1581 Italian scientist Galileo Galilei observes the regularity of a pendulum's swing.

Pendulum clock designed by Galileo

1657 Huygens builds the first pendulum clock.

1759 Englishman John Harrison makes a marine timekeeper, or chronometer, that has less than one minute of error after five months at sea.

Harrison's chronometer

1884 The time at Greenwich, London, UK, is adopted as the standard time for the whole world.

1905 Einstein's Special Theory of Relativity gives a new understanding of the concept of time.

1929 Warren Morrison, an American, invents the quartz clock.

1948 The atomic clock is developed in the USA.

1965 US physicists Arno Penzias and Robert Wilson provide evidence that time began with the Big Bang.

FIND OUT MORE ATOMS AND MOLECULES · AZTECS · BLACK HOLES · CHINA, HISTORY OF · CRYSTALS AND GEMS · EINSTEIN, ALBERT · FORCE AND MOTION · GALILEO GALILEI · PHYSICS · SUN AND SOLAR SYSTEM

Time

Early time pieces

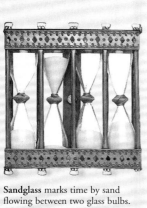

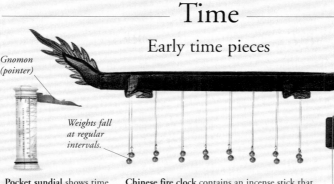

Gnomon (pointer)

Weights fall at regular intervals.

Holes for pin

Position of pin was changed according to time of year.

Plumbline

Ornamental handle.

Sandglass marks time by sand flowing between two glass bulbs.

Pocket sundial shows time by gnomon's shadow.

Chinese fire clock contains an incense stick that releases weights as it burns through the threads.

Merkhet, from ancient Egypt, traced movement of stars across the sky.

Tibetan timestick used pin's shadow to tell time.

Historical clocks and watches

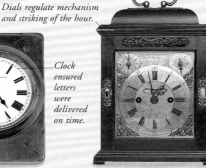

Carrying handle

Watch could be hung from a chain attached to a button-hole.

Dials regulate mechanism and striking of the hour.

Clock ensured letters were delivered on time.

Carriage clocks were portable clocks used by travellers.

Pocket watch, 18th century

Mail clock, 19th century, for keeping time on mail trains.

Bracket clock, 17th century, stood on table or mantlepiece.

Swinging pendulum bob

Falling weight drives hands.

Bird emerges with cry of "cuckoo!" every hour.

Wooden case gave clock a loud "tick-tock" sound.

Clock regulated by moving small weights along a bar.

Outer dial shows minutes.

Verge watch, driven by a coiled spring

Pendulum clocks were controlled by the swing of a suspended weight.

Cuckoo clocks were invented in Germany around 1730.

Grandfather clocks housed pendulum in a long case.

Lantern clocks were named after their lantern-like shape.

Japanese ornamental clock, made out of the gemstone turquoise.

Modern clocks and watches

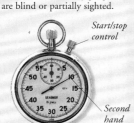

Braille watch used by people who are blind or partially sighted.

Dial shows diver's time under water.

Friendly panda

Talking watch speaks the time to the wearer.

Start/stop control

Second hand

Rubber strap

Display shows time as digits.

Upside-down face

Stopwatch can measure time in fractions of a second.

Mechanical alarm clock rings bells at pre-set time.

Waterproof watch for use by divers

Child's clock has large hands and clear numbers.

Digital alarm clock controlled by a tiny quartz crystal

Nurse's watch hangs from nurse's uniform.

TRADE AND INDUSTRY

ANY SORT OF ACTIVITY that is done to create wealth is known as industry. The term also describes a group of businesses that produce a similar service or provide a similar product. Trade is the process of buying and selling such products. The thousands of different industries do many things, such as mining, advertising, construction, farming, and broadcasting. Many industries change raw materials into products. Others provide services, from haircuts to health care.

Coal is an important fuel in industry; most of the world's supply is mined in Asia.

Primary industry
Coal, oil, stone, cereal crops, and timber are among the products of primary industry, which is concerned with extracting raw materials from the Earth. Such products may be used just as they are, or processed by the manufacturing industries into something else.

Types of industry

When most people talk about industry, they are thinking of the factories and assembly lines involved in manufacturing. In fact, there are three basic types of industry: primary, manufacturing, and service industries. In the developing countries, most people work in primary industry. Any country where most people work in the manufacturing and service industries is known as an industrialized nation.

Car manufacture

Manufacturing
The manufacturing, or secondary, industries make products either from raw materials or from other manufactured goods. Much modern manufacturing is heavily automated: machines carry out the heavy, repetitive tasks.

Service
The service, or tertiary, industries do not produce anything, but offer a service, such as banking. In some highly industrialized countries, more people work in service industries than in either of the other industries.

Service industries include restaurants, shops, and tourist businesses.

Restaurant in Paris

What industry needs

In order for an industry to produce anything, it must have certain basic assets: money, machinery, labour, and raw materials. The aim of any industry is to make a profit. If the basic assets are abundant and inexpensive, then the industry produces a more profitable product or service. An industry also needs a market: if nobody wants to buy a product, the money and effort spent in making it is wasted.

Washing powder

Soap

Dishwashing liquid

Detergents, products of chemical industry

Violin maker

Cottage industry
Cottage industry is where workers produce goods on a small scale, generally in the home or a small workshop. The workers may sell the goods themselves, or to an employer who pays per finished piece. The system may be abused by unscrupulous employers, who pay low rates for long hours.

Energy and materials
Both the primary and manufacturing industries must have materials to work with, and fuels and energy to power machines. In some countries, large industrialized regions, such as the Ruhr in Germany, develop near areas of raw materials, such as coal or iron ore.

Coal mines

Oil

Timber

Steel

Raw materials and fuels

The service industries depend most heavily on labour.

Stages in production
In the manufacturing industry, most products go through basic stages before they can be sold to the public. Once the product is designed, the design is checked to ensure that the product works and is affordable. The product is made from raw materials; finally, it is tested, to make sure there are no faults.

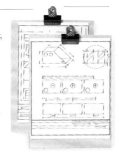

Product designs

Factory premises

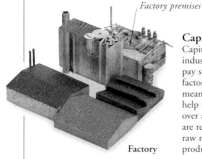

Capital
Capital means money, which industries need to buy machinery, pay staff, and build or rent a factory or other premises. It also means the equipment that will help to manufacture a product over a period of time. Machines are regarded as capital, but the raw materials from which products are made are not.

Factory

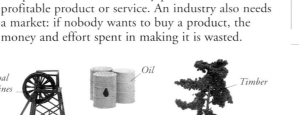

Labour
Many industries are set up close to cities, so they can have a ready supply of workers, or labour. The labour supply must include management, accountants, and research and development staff among others, plus manual workers.

Communications
Good communications are vital for the growth of industry. Efficient road systems, railways, air and sea routes, and global telecommunications allow some industries to make their goods in parts of the world where property prices and wages are lower.

Trade

The process of exchanging the goods or services produced by industry is known as trade. It is a vital part of modern life. Even the richest nations do not have the resources to produce everything their people need or want; by trading surplus goods with others, countries earn the money to buy the things they need. Trade between different countries is called foreign trade. So-called domestic trade takes place within the boundaries of a country.

Market traders, 15th century

History of trade

Trade has an ancient history. From about 3000 BC, the Phoenicians traded metals, cloth, and animals with Mediterranean peoples. From 300 BC, traders travelled the Silk Road from China to Europe, a famous early trade route. Trade between different peoples led to the exchange of ideas and culture, as well as goods. Trade between different countries grew steadily from medieval times on, when merchants travelled the globe with goods.

Distribution

The movement of goods or services from the manufacturer to the consumer (the person who wants to buy them) is known as distribution. Distribution between producer, wholesaler, and retailer relies on efficient, economical transport systems. International trade has grown steadily, partly thanks to advances in transportation – for example, the arrival of the railways, air freight, and refrigerated cargo ships.

Refrigerated warehouse

Wholesalers

Many small shops rely on wholesalers to deliver products to them when needed. A wholesaler is a business that buys large quantities of goods directly from the manufacturers. It stores them in huge warehouses, ready to sell in smaller amounts at higher prices to retail outlets, or shops. Warehouses are found near major roads or railways, to ensure rapid, economical transport of the products.

Retailers

Retailers are businesses that buy products from wholesalers and sell them at a higher price. Most high-street shops are part of the retail trade – a place where consumers can buy the goods they want. As such, shops are the end of a long chain of trading.

Buying jeans from a shop

Imports and exports

The goods or services one country buys from another are called imports; the goods a country sells to others are called exports. To earn the money to pay for imports, a country must export its own produce.

Imports   Exports

Goods coming in   *Goods going out*

Balance of payments

The payments a country makes to others for imported goods, and the payments it receives from other countries for exports within the same period of time, are together known as the balance of payments. If a country does not export enough goods, it must borrow money to pay for imports.

Tariffs and customs

Some countries tax imported goods. This tax is known as a customs duty, or tariff. Such duties are a way of making money for the government, or of protecting the country's industries by raising the price of imported goods, which might otherwise be cheaper than those produced locally.

World trade

International trade is regulated by the World Trade Organization, set up in 1995. It works to reduce trade barriers and tariffs between nations. It succeeded the General Agreement on Tariffs and Trade (GATT), set up in 1948 under the auspices of the United Nations.

World Trade Organization building

Factory chimneys

Industrial pollution

Industry provides us with clothing, food, shelter, labour-saving devices, and medicines. But it has harmful side effects. Many industrial processes cause pollution in the form of smoke from factories, and waste products dumped in the sea, rivers, and lakes. The rapid growth of industry threatens to exhaust the world's supplies of oil and natural gas.

Werner von Siemens

German engineer Werner von Siemens (1816–92) helped the growth of the communications industry, by his improvements to the telegraph. The electrical manufacturer AG Siemens, which trades in more than 125 countries, evolved from a company originally established by the Siemens family.

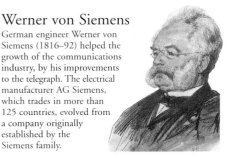

Timeline

c.3000 BC Phoenicians trade with other countries around the Mediterranean.

c.1500 Commercial Revolution begins; merchants start trading around the globe.

Newcomen's engine

1705 English inventor Thomas Newcomen (1663–1729) builds a simple steam engine that contributes to the 18th-century Industrial Revolution in Great Britain.

1871 Trade Union Act makes trade unions legal in Britain.

1913 US industrialist Henry Ford (1863–1947) introduces assembly-line procedures to produce his Model-T cars, stimulating mass-production.

20th century Transport and communications developments spur growth of foreign trade.

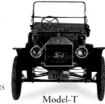

Model-T

1968 The European Economic Community (EEC) abandons trade tariffs between member nations, establishing a "Common Market".

1990s USA, Japan, and European nations are the world's major traders.

FIND OUT MORE ADVERTISING AND MARKETING · FARMING · FISHING INDUSTRY · INDUSTRIAL REVOLUTION · MONEY · POLLUTION · PORTS AND WATERWAYS · SHOPS · TRANSPORT, HISTORY OF · UNIONS, TRADE

TRAINS AND RAILWAYS

WHEN YOU SEE a sleek express train whizzing by, you may find it hard to believe that the first railways were iron tracks with wooden wagons pulled by horses. The first steam railways were opened in the 1820s, allowing people and goods to travel at undreamed-of speeds. The new form of transport spread rapidly across the world. Today's trains are a very efficient method of transport – they use less fuel and produce less pollution than cars and trucks, and carry much larger cargos. Many people believe trains are the best form of transport for the future.

Early trains

The first train provided passengers with a bumpy ride on wooden seats in open goods wagons designed to carry coal. At the front of the train was a steam-powered locomotive, which pulled the wagons not much faster than walking pace. Some trains towed wagons onto which the passengers attached their own carriages.

Wheels are driven by steam-powered pistons

"Catch Me Who Can", built in 1808

Bullet train
Japanese Shinkansen, or "bullet" trains, travel along specially built high-speed tracks. They average speeds up to 225 kmh (140 mph). Other countries have also opened new lines designed for high-speed electric trains, including France, where the TGV train holds the world speed record of more than 500 kmh (310 mph).

Electric locomotive gets its electricity via a catenary (overhead cable system).

Bullet trains first ran in 1965.

Modern trains

Electricity and engines powered by diesel make modern trains move. In an electric locomotive, electric motors turn the wheels. The electricity comes from the track or from overhead cables. In a diesel-electric locomotive, a powerful diesel engine turns an electric generator. This creates electricity, which in turn drives electric motors. Modern carriages give a smooth, comfortable ride and are air-conditioned. They have automatic locking doors for the safety of their passengers.

Overhead cables for electric locomotives

Gantries support cables and signals.

Points are intersections in the rails that move trains onto a new section of track.

Signals keep trains a safe distance apart.

Tracks

Railway tracks have two parallel steel rails supported on wood or concrete sleepers which spread the weight of passing trains into the ground. Rails are often welded into a continuous track to allow trains to run smoothly. Points direct trains left or right on to diverging tracks. Most railways have different tracks for opposite directions.

George Stephenson

British railway engineer George Stephenson (1781–1848) established his locomotive works in 1823 and built the very first public railway, from Stockton to Darlington, England, in 1825. He also built many steam locomotives, working with his son Robert.

Trams

Many cities, especially in Europe, have a tram system. Trams run on railway tracks laid in the streets. They are usually powered by electricity from overhead wires.

Types of train

A train consists of locomotives and rolling stock (carriages and goods wagons for freight). Commuter trains and local trains, which make many stops and starts, often have combined locomotives and carriages, called multiple units. Sleeper trains travel long distances and have bunk beds for passengers.

Passenger express
Express trains usually have a separate locomotive at the front. The rolling stock often includes a buffet car for snacks and drinks and a dining car, as well as normal carriages with seats. Some high-speed trains have a locomotive at each end.

Goods train
A long goods train can have hundreds of trucks, and sometimes more than one locomotive. Some trucks are designed to hold specific cargoes, such as oil tankers.

Hong Kong trams
Double-decker trams have been running through the streets of Hong Kong for many decades. They provide a clean form of transport that is needed in a crowded city. Trams were taken out of some cities in the mid-20th century, but efficient new tram systems are now being built in their place.

FIND OUT MORE   CARS AND TRUCKS   ENERGY   ENGINES AND MOTORS   FORCE AND MOTION   INDUSTRIAL REVOLUTION   TRANSPORT, HISTORY OF   TRAVEL

TRANSPORT, HISTORY OF

FROM SIMPLE, PREHISTORIC rafts to the arrival of supersonic passenger flight, transport has a long history. For centuries, the only way to move around on land was to walk or to use animals as beasts of burden. The invention of the wheel around 3500 BC, and the ensuing development of wheeled vehicles, revolutionized transport. Also important was the arrival of powered vehicles, with the development of steam engines in the 18th century, and the internal combustion engine in the late 19th century.

Cast-iron spokes with wooden rim

Wire spoked wheel

Strong and light metal alloy wheel

Wheels
The most important invention in transport history was the wheel. Draught animals could pull wheeled vehicles with heavy loads for far longer than they could drag or carry the same load. Wheels were solid wood until spokes were developed in about 2,000 BC. Tyres were originally made from iron. Pneumatic tyres, filled with air and made of rubber to cushion the ride, appeared in the 1890s.

Carts and carriages
People travelled on early roads in two-wheeled carts and four-wheeled wagons or carriages. These were pulled by horses or oxen. "Horseless carriages" – carriages powered by steam engines – were first made in the 18th century.

Road transport

Roads began as footpaths that often meandered around the contours of the countryside. Then 2,000 years ago, Roman engineers built a vast network of straight roads that allowed people, goods, and troops to move quickly across their empire. Few new roads were built until the 18th century, when they were needed for mail coaches. In the 20th century, roads carrying several lanes of traffic crisscrossed the landscape as car ownership became widespread.

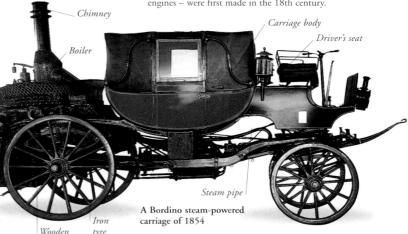

Chimney

Boiler

Carriage body

Driver's seat

Steam pipe

Wooden spoke

Iron tyre

A Bordino steam-powered carriage of 1854

Cars
Experimental motor cars were built soon after the invention of the internal combustion engine, which was compact enough to be carried around, in 1876. In 1886, the first practical motor car was demonstrated to the public. Today, the car is the most common form of transport in many countries.

The Toyota 2000GT Japan; launched 1966; top speed 206 kmh (128 mph); a classic small sports car.

Trucks
The first trucks appeared in the 1890s. Powered by steam engines, they began to replace heavy, horse-drawn carts for road haulage. Most modern trucks have powerful diesel engines. There are many specialized trucks for carrying different types of cargo, such as cars, liquids, or refrigerated foods.

Modern articulated truck

Kiichiro Toyoda
Japanese engineer Kiichiro Toyoda (1894–1952), established the Toyota Motor Corporation in 1937. He devoted much of his life to producing affordable passenger cars, and to building up a vast manufacturing company.

Rail transport

An important development in transport history came in 1804, when the first steam locomotive was built to run on rails. Passenger railways opened in the 1820s – the first fast form of land travel. Steam power lasted until the mid-20th century, when it was replaced by electric motors or diesel engines.

Modern trains
Electric current to power trains comes from the tracks or overhead cables. High-speed, long-distance trains are sleek and give a smooth, comfortable ride in air-conditioned carriages: an example is the Eurostar, which travels from London, England to Paris, France in a few hours. Local commuter trains carry thousands of people into and out of towns and cities every day.

Bicycles
The first type of bicycle was the Draisine of 1817. It had no pedals, but was pushed along by the rider's feet. Pedals attached to the front wheel appeared in 1839 and were improved upon in 1865. The modern-style bicycle, where the pedals drive the back wheel with a chain, was developed in the 1880s. Bicycles are a popular form of transport, especially on flat land, but in many countries they are now used mainly for leisure. In some parts of the world, such as China, most people still travel by bike.

Modern mountain bike

Early trains
Passengers on early trains travelled in uncomfortable open wagons pulled by slow, puffing steam locomotives. Steam engines gradually became more powerful and rolling stock more comfortable. By the end of the 1800s, steam locomotives were pulling express trains at more than 150 kmh (93 mph).

An electric-powered Eurostar express train waiting to leave its London terminus

Water transport

Travelling on water is one of the oldest forms of transport. The earliest craft were simple rafts made of logs lashed together. In the ancient civilizations of Egypt and Mesopotamia, people built boats from bundled reeds to travel up and down river. They also built wooden sea-going ships and used them for trading. Until the advent of the railways in the 1800s, boats and ships were the only way of transporting heavy goods over long distances. Today, there are various types of boats and ships made from many materials, from bark and animal skins to plastic, fibreglass, iron, and steel.

Queen Elizabeth II ocean liner

Steam and iron

In the 1800s, steam power began to replace sail. This freed ships from relying on the wind. At the same time, shipbuilders began to use huge plates of iron riveted together to construct hulls. This allowed them to build much bigger ships than was possible with wood. Huge luxurious passenger liners were built, which rivalled the best hotels on land.

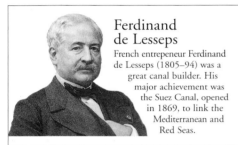

Ferdinand de Lesseps

French entrepeneur Ferdinand de Lesseps (1805–94) was a great canal builder. His major achievement was the Suez Canal, opened in 1869, to link the Mediterranean and Red Seas.

Sail

The first sailing ships, built in about 3500 BC, had simple square sails. These were well suited for sailing with the wind behind, but oars were needed to go against the wind. From the 1600s, ships had both square and triangular sails. The triangular sail, or lateen, could be used for tacking – sailing in a zig-zag pattern to make headway into the wind. The sailing ship ushered in an age of worldwide exploration and trade.

Traditional bargeware is still to be seen on today's pleasure barges.

Decorated bargeware used on canal boats in the 19th century

Wooden masts support sails

Cloth sails stiffened with thin wooden spars

Chinese junk with lateen sails

Hull of wooden planking

Sternpost rudder for steering

Canals

Before the development of trains and trucks, heavy goods were transported from place to place via networks of purpose-built waterways, called canals. Cargoes were carried by flat-bottomed boats, called barges. Some shipping canals, such as Suez and Panama, were built to shorten sea routes by cutting across narrow strips of land. Today, though barges are still used for transporting goods, they are also popular for leisure trips.

Air transport

The first powered aeroplane flight was made in 1903. Airmail and passenger services began after World War I. Air travel has since developed into an everyday form of transport for passengers and goods.

Passenger travel

The first airliners were converted World War I bombers. Long-distance air travel really took off in the 1920s and 1930s with the development of all-metal airliners and huge flying boats driven by piston engines. Jet-powered airliners, such as the Boeing 707, were put into service in the 1950s, making air travel faster, quieter, and cheaper. The introduction of the wide-bodied jet in 1970 makes international jet travel commonplace.

Balloons and airships

The first manned flight was made in a hot-air balloon; but balloons are blown by the wind, and cannot be steered. By the 1920s, airships powered by engines carried passengers across the Atlantic. Filled with hydrogen, they were at terrible risk from fire.

Helicopters

Developed by many aircraft engineers through the 20th century, helicopters were first produced in large numbers in the 1940s. Unlike most other aircraft, they do not need a runway for take-off and landing, and can hover over the same spot. This makes them invaluable for fast transport to inaccessible places, and for rescue, police, and military work.

The helicopter's rotors are powered by a turbo-shaft jet engine.

Timeline

1804 Richard Trevithick builds first steam-powered railway locomotive.

1825 Stockton to Darlington Railway in England is the first public railway to start operations.

The Ordinary bicycle, nicknamed the "penny farthing"

1838 The steamship *Great Western* begins a regular transatlantic passenger service.

1874 In Britain, the Ordinary bicycle is invented. It has a massive front wheel, to make it as fast as possible, and a small rear wheel for balance.

1886 In Germany, the first petrol-engined car – a three-wheeled vehicle – makes its first public run.

1903 In the USA, the Wright brothers make the first successful aeroplane flight in their *Flyer*.

Henry Ford's Model T

1908 Introduction of the Model T Ford, the first small economy car to be mass produced.

1952 Jet-powered passenger services begin in the De Havilland Comet operated by British airline BOAC.

 FIND OUT MORE AIRCRAFT • AIRSHIPS AND BALLOONS • BICYCLES AND MOTORCYCLES • CARS AND TRUCKS • EXPLORATION • FLIGHT, HISTORY OF • PORTS AND WATERWAYS • SHIPS AND BOATS • TRAINS AND RAILWAYS

TRAVEL

PEOPLE HAVE BEEN on the move since prehistoric times: initially to find food or territory, and then for trade, exploration, and pleasure. Some have travelled great distances to escape danger or oppression. However, it is only since the 19th century, with the advent of new, efficient methods of transport, that mass travel has become widely available. In 1990, there were 425 million tourists worldwide.

Early travel
The ancient Romans visited thermal spas for their health, medieval pilgrims travelled great distances to reach religious shrines, and in 18th-century Europe young aristocrats made the "Grand Tour", visiting sites of classical antiquity. Before the advent of modern transport, travel was a gruelling experience. People covered vast distances on foot, often across lonely, wild landscapes, and at risk from bandits and wild animals. Only the rich could afford to travel in comfort.

Thermal bath, England

Tourism

Tourism has become the world's biggest industry as more and more people travel away from home for short periods of time. Although most people go to see family and friends, or to explore a new country, others may take short breaks to health spas, or take part in study tours. People also travel to attend business meetings.

Seaside holidays
In 18th-century England, trips to the seaside were a pastime taken up by the wealthy. By the 1840s, better social conditions marked the start of affordable holidays for the working class, who flocked to the seaside by train. Today, Europeans and North Americans take the most holidays to seaside resorts around the world.

Travel agents
The first travel agency opened in the 1850s. Since then, a large industry has developed devoted to organizing tours, booking tickets and hotels, and insuring holidaymakers.

Thomas Cook
Baptist missionary, Thomas Cook (1808–92) started a career in tourism in 1841, when he set up a train service for a party of missionaries. By 1855 he was organizing trips to the Paris Exposition, running the "Grand Tour" of Europe, and establishing the world's first travel agency.

Migration

Over the centuries people have been leaving their country of origin, searching for a better life, escaping famine, warfare, or hardship. Between 1892 and 1954, the United States saw the greatest wave of migration ever, when nearly 17 million people arrived in New York before settling in other parts of the country. Other popular destinations for people seeking a new life include Australia.

Statue of Liberty welcoming new arrivals to New York

Holidays today

Package holidays, which offer flights and hotels at bargain rates, are extremely popular. Increasingly, people are looking to remote corners of the globe to find undiscovered holiday destinations, while tour operators compete to meet this demand.

Tourists visiting pyramids in Egypt

Refugees
Famine, war, and conflict have displaced millions of people, driving them from their homes. They are forced to find asylum, or refuge, in other countries, and if they fail to do so, may remain stateless. Often refugees have to leave their homes quickly and only take the personal possessions they can carry on their backs. During the 1980s, the plight of refugees was highlighted by the Vietnamese boat people who fled their country in fear of persecution.

Ecotourism
Regions that have interesting wildlife, such as Antarctica, have become holiday destinations for nature-lovers. Specialized travel companies provide organized tours to these remote parts of the world, little seen by other tourists. However, this kind of tourism can have a terrible impact on fragile ecosystems. The 1990s have seen a move towards responsible ecotourism, protecting the rare environments on which it depends.

A rucksack can hold everything a backpacker needs, such as a sleeping bag and camping equipment.

Backpacking
Many people prefer independent travel to organized tourism, especially young people travelling on a tight budget for long periods of time. Backpackers like to take very little luggage, and they travel cheaply by using local transport, camping, and buying food in local stores. In this way, it is possible to explore remote and exotic regions that have not been reached by other tourists.

TREES

FOR MORE THAN 210 million years, trees have flourished on Earth. The earliest trees were giant, woody, spore-producing plants that were the ancestors of ferns and clubmosses. Today's trees are large seed-producing plants with a single upright woody stem called a trunk. Trees help to balance the atmosphere, stabilize the soil, supply all kinds of creatures with food, and produce wood for people to use. They fall into three groups: conifers, broad-leaved trees, and palms. Trees can live for a very long time; many species survive for 200 years, and the bristlecone pine can live for 4,000 years.

The top of a tree is called the crown.

Each spring, twigs, leaves, and flowers develop from buds.

As a tree grows taller, many twigs are shed, and only a few grow into branches.

Higher up the tree, the bark is often smooth and pale in colour.

The bark is thicker and darker near the base of the trunk, and is cracked into ridges, called plates.

The tangled network of roots spreads out horizontally as well as down into the soil.

Profile of an oak tree

How a tree grows

Each year the tree's crown grows a little taller and broader. The twigs and side shoots grow longer only from their tips. The branches and trunk become thicker as the layer of cells called the cambium divides. This process is called secondary thickening. A ring of growth called an annual ring is formed each year.

Tree trunks

Most of the tree trunk consists of wood, which is a very tough, durable material. Wood is rigid and strong, yet so flexible that the tree trunk can support the weight of the crown and sway in the wind without snapping.

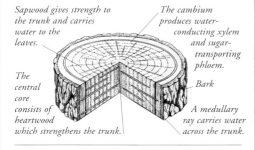

Sapwood gives strength to the trunk and carries water to the leaves.

The cambium produces water-conducting xylem and sugar-transporting phloem.

The central core consists of heartwood which strengthens the trunk.

Bark

A medullary ray carries water across the trunk.

Bark

Covering the trunk and branches is a layer of corky, waterproof bark. Beneath this is the layer called the phloem. The bark helps to protect the living phloem from hot and cold temperature extremes, and it also helps to stop insect and fungal pests from damaging the tree.

Poplar bark is cracked into vertical ridges.

River birch bark peels off the trunk in uneven flakes.

Himalayan birch peels in long, horizontal strips.

Parts of a tree

A tree consists of a trunk that supports a crown of branches, and roots that anchor the tree into the ground and absorb water and minerals from the soil. Water passes up the trunk from the roots, and sugars are carried to the roots from the leaves. The branches bear leaves, flowers, fruits, or cones.

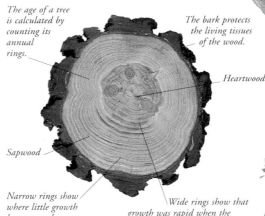

The age of a tree is calculated by counting its annual rings.

The bark protects the living tissues of the wood.

Heartwood

Sapwood

Narrow rings show where little growth has occurred.

Wide rings show that growth was rapid when the conditions were good.

Tallest trees

The tallest living coniferous tree in the world is the "National Geographic Society" coast redwood in North America, which has reached more than 111 m (364 ft) high. The tallest broad-leaved species of tree is the Australian mountain ash. This has been known to grow up to 113 m (370 ft) high.

Coniferous trees

All conifers are either tall trees or woody shrubs, and they are almost all evergreen. They belong to a group of flowerless plants called gymnosperms. The seeds of conifers are not enclosed inside fruits. Instead, they either develop between the woody scales of cones, or they are embedded in a fleshy cup or scale.

Cones open in warm weather to release their seeds.

Cones
Female pine cones are woody, and some are extremely hard, with sharp prickles at the tip of each scale. Male cones produce large amounts of pollen, then fall from the tree. The pollen is carried to the female cones by the wind.

Cone shapes
Cones may be round, ovoid, or cylindrical. They range in size from the 1 cm (0.4 in) cones of some cypresses to the 60 cm (24 in)-long cone of the sugar pine. The heavy cones of the big cone pine tree may weigh up to 2.27 kg (5 lb).

Norway spruce cone

Pine trees
There are about 80 species of pine tree. All except one grow in the northern hemisphere. Pine trees are typical conifers. Their seeds develop inside hard pine cones. Pine leaves are narrow needles that grow in clusters and give off a pleasant, distinctive smell.

Pine tree

Needles
Pine trees have long, narrow, spiky needles that stay on the tree for at least two years. These needles are arranged in bunches of two, three, or five.

Douglas fir cone

Redwood cone

Conifers in winter
Evergreen conifers keep their needles all winter. A thick, waxy outer layer on the needles prevents frost from harming them. The branches of conifers curve downwards so that snow slides easily off their crowns.

Resin
The roots, leaves, and trunk of conifers ooze sticky resins when the tree is cut or damaged. This resin helps to seal the wound, keeping out harmful insects and fungal spores. Resin can be tapped and used to make turpentine.

Tree shapes
Each type of tree has a certain shape. Broad-leaved trees usually have a spreading crown, whereas conifers often have a spire shape. Palms usually have a tuft of large, feathery leaves.

Broad-leaved tree **Conifer** **Palm**

Broad-leaved trees

This is the largest group of living trees, with more than 10,000 different species. Broad-leaved trees have thin, flat leaves on a spreading crown of irregular branches. Many broad-leaved trees are deciduous, shedding their leaves each autumn.

Each acorn sits in a little cup.

Acorns
The fruit of an oak tree is a one-seeded nut called an acorn. A large oak may produce thousands of acorns in a single season. Only a small amount germinate, and even fewer survive to grow into trees.

Oak trees
Oaks are typical broad-leaved trees. There are about 800 species. Oak wood is very hard and durable, so many types of oak tree are commercially important, providing valuable timber for building and furniture making.

Buds
Tightly folded inside each bud are the soft leaves of the next season's growth. Tough scales protect these buds and are shed as soon as the bud starts to open.

Leaves are grouped in clusters at the tips of the twigs.

Leaves
Broad, flat leaves have a large surface area, which makes them efficient at producing food for the tree. They are also easily damaged by wind and insects because they are thin. To deter insects, these leaves often contain unpleasant tasting substances, such as the bitter tannins in oaks.

Oak tree

How trees lose their leaves

1 Chlorophyll in the leaf starts to break down, and the tree reabsorbs nutrients.

2 Waste products enter the dying leaf, which provides a useful disposal system for the tree.

3 These chemical changes make the leaf change colour, creating the brilliant reds and golds of autumn.

4 Before a leaf is shed, a corky layer forms across the base of the leaf stalk. The leaf snaps off at this point, leaving a scar.

Leaf scar

Bud

Palm trees
Most palm trees grow in tropical or sub-tropical regions. Many have a tall, woody trunk without branches. The large leaves, called fronds, grow in a fan-like tuft on the upper part of the trunk.

The sago palm tree has a seed that is enclosed in a corky fruit covered with overlapping scales.

FIND OUT MORE   FORESTS   FRUITS AND SEEDS   FURNITURE   PHOTOSYNTHESIS   PLANTS   PLANTS, ANATOMY   PLANT USES   RAINFOREST WILDLIFE   WOODLAND WILDLIFE

Trees
Conifers

Male cone

Leaves have two white bands on the underside.

Cone consists of six overlapping scales.

Scalelike leaves

Monkey puzzle has stiff, sharp, triangular leaves. It grows naturally on the slopes of the Andes in South America.

Plum-fruited yew is a South American tree, not related to true yews. Its seeds are encased in an edible fleshy scale.

Incense cedar is a tall, narrow tree from North America. Its wood has a pleasant smell.

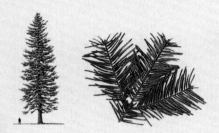

Egg-shaped upright cone

Giant fir is a 164 ft (150 m) tall tree of the damp coastal forests of the Pacific Northwest.

Stone pine grows all around the Mediterranean region. It has large, heavy cones full of edible seeds.

Japanese larch is one of the few deciduous conifers. It is an important tree for the timber industry.

Broad-leaved trees

A single brown nut is enclosed inside the fruit.

Leaves have ten or fewer pairs of veins.

Bristly fruit husk

Black walnut has large edible seeds and provides one of the most highly valued timbers in the world.

Silver birch is a graceful, white-barked tree. It quickly grows in open spaces. Flowers are borne in catkins.

Common beech is a valuable timber tree, with dense foliage that provides thick shade.

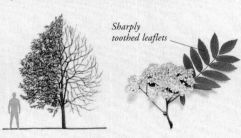

Fruit, called an acorn, is held in a rough cup.

Sharply toothed leaflets

Leaves turn yellow to orange or red in fall.

White oak has large, lobed leaves that turn a brilliant purplish red in fall. It grows in eastern North America.

Mountain ash has clusters of small flowers followed by orange-red berries much loved by birds.

Sugar maple is also known as rock maple. It is tapped for its sap, which is then refined into maple syrup.

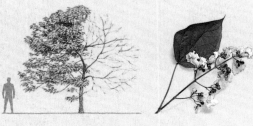

Cider gum is one of about 600 different kinds of eucalyptus trees from Australia.

Indian bean tree grows in moist places in the southeastern US. It has long narrow seedpods.

White poplar has foliage so thickly covered with cottony down when it is young that the leaves look white.

T

TRUTH, SOJOURNER

IN THE 19TH CENTURY, most black people in America were slaves, and black women had no rights at all. One remarkable woman dedicated her life to changing this situation. Sojourner Truth was born a slave, but was freed and spent her free life campaigning against slavery and fighting for women's rights. Her speeches and actions gave heart to all those who fought to abolish slavery, and inspired many early feminists.

Early life

Isabella Baumfree was born the daughter of two slaves in New York State, USA, in about 1797 – her owner did not record the year. Her parents died in 1809 and she was bought and sold several times. In 1826 she escaped from her owners, and was freed from slavery on 4 July 1827, when all slaves in New York State who had been born before 4 July 1799 were freed. Isabella took the name Sojourner Truth in 1843.

Campaigns

As soon as she gained her freedom in 1827, Isabella (as she was then known) began to fight against slavery. She gave support to the anti-slavery Union side in the US Civil War, especially to the black soldiers who fought in the war. She also cared for freed slaves, nursing them when they were ill, and helping to educate them. Throughout her life she travelled around the country, preaching the word of God, campaigning against the evils of slavery, and speaking in support of women's rights. She set an example that has been followed by black activists to the present day.

Speaking and preaching

Truth spent much of her life as a travelling preacher, paying her way by doing domestic work for the people who came to hear her speak. Although she could neither read nor write, she knew much of the Bible by heart. She was an electrifying platform performer and became a household name in the USA.

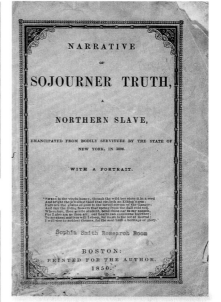

Narrative

In 1850, Sojourner Truth published her autobiography, *Narrative of Sojourner Truth*. This was a rare accomplishment for a black woman at that time, especially since Truth had never learned to read or write. She had to dictate the book to a friend. The book was successful and sold many copies, giving Sojourner Truth an income which she used to travel around the country on her campaigns against slavery.

Women's rights

As a black woman, Sojourner Truth had to face extreme prejudice on account of both her race and her sex. But this only reinforced her conviction that she was the equal of any man, and she, therefore, campaigned for women to be given equal status in American society. Although there were numerous campaigns for women's rights in the USA in the 19th century, most of them were organized by white women, some of whom did not accept Sojourner Truth, a black ex-slave, as their equal.

Poster for lecture

Meeting of women's rights campaigners

The war effort

During the American Civil War of 1861–65, Sojourner Truth made a tour of the midwestern states to get support for the anti-slavery Union cause. She met with great hostility in some of the places she visited. In one town an anti-war group threatened to burn down the hall where she was speaking. The threat did not deter Sojourner Truth. She retorted to the protesters: "Then I will speak upon its ashes".

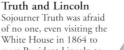

Cavalry officer / *Foot soldiers of the 58th regiment*

Memorial to black Civil War Regiment

Truth and Lincoln

Sojourner Truth was afraid of no one, even visiting the White House in 1864 to meet President Lincoln to persuade him to support her various causes. When she said that she had not heard of him before he was president, he replied that he had heard of her years ago.

Truth with Lincoln

SOJOURNER TRUTH

c.1797	Born in Hurley, New York State, USA.
1809	Parents Betsy and James die.
1826	Escapes from her owners.
1827	Granted her freedom on Freedom Day.
1843	Takes the name Sojourner Truth.
1850	*Narrative of Sojourner Truth* published.
1862	Supports anti-slavery side in US Civil War.
1883	Dies at Battle Creek, Michigan.

FIND OUT MORE

AMERICAN CIVIL WAR · HUMAN RIGHTS · KING, MARTIN LUTHER · SLAVERY · SOCIETIES, HUMAN · UNITED STATES, HISTORY OF · WOMEN'S MOVEMENT

TUNDRA

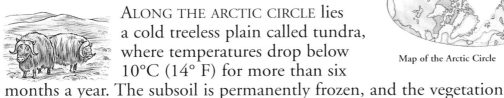

ALONG THE ARCTIC CIRCLE lies a cold treeless plain called tundra, where temperatures drop below 10°C (14° F) for more than six months a year. The subsoil is permanently frozen, and the vegetation is restricted to mosses, lichen, sedges, and rushes, with occasional flowers and small deciduous shrubs, such as hazel and alder. Animals include the Arctic fox and snowshoe rabbit. Worn flat by the vast ice sheets of the past, the tundra is now an open landscape of shallow lakes, bare rock outcrops, and small hummocks.

Map of the Arctic Circle

Tundra regions

Tundra exists mostly within the Arctic Circle. There are also tundra regions in the far north of Alaska, Canada, Scandinavia, and Siberia. It is widest in North Siberia, on the Kara Sea, and reaches as far south as the Kamchatka peninsula.

Tundra

Tundra landscape

Frequently covered in snow and ice, the ground in the tundra landscape is so cold that in many places it is permanently frozen. This is called permafrost. The occasional melting of the ice in the ground above the permafrost level causes "cryoturbation", a stirring up of the ground that creates a unique range of landforms.

Periglacial activity

The landscapes bordering ice sheets are periglacial (near glacial). The bitterly cold conditions produce a distinctive environment. All tundra is periglacial, as are nunataks and hills in ice sheets. In winter, the temperature never rises above freezing, and often drops to -50°C (-58°F). Short, mild summers allow the ice to melt.

Periglacial landscape

Stone stripes

In periglacial areas, water freezing in between stones in the ground heaves the stones upwards in places, creating stone patterns – stone stripes and rings called stone polygons.

Sparse vegetation

Frozen ground often cracks. Meltwater fills these cracks, and expands to create ice wedges.

Lake

Ice beneath the ground creates pingos.

New ice wedge

Nunataks

Conditions and landforms on nunataks, upland areas protruding above the ice sheet, are very similar to those in the tundra. However, nunataks are cut off by vast seas of ice, so they are often completely bare of vegetation and animal life, and the ground is unprotected.

Topsoil defrosts during short summer months.

Mother rock

When ice in frozen soil melts, it makes the soil so fluid that it slumps down the gentlest of slopes.

Sediments are twisted by cryoturbation into buckled layers called involutions.

Permanently frozen subsoil

Ice wedge filled with gravel

Mammoth

Permafrost has been frozen for thousands of years. It sometimes contains the perfectly preserved remains of long extinct animals, including complete carcasses of mammoths that died out over 10,000 years ago. This mammoth was found frozen in Siberia.

Pingos

These are mounds up to 50 m (160 ft) high which have been raised by the freezing and expansion of their ice core. The ice core may once have been a shallow lake that filled up with sediment, or it may be frozen groundwater. As the core melts, the pingo collapses.

Permafrost

Unfrozen ground

Permafrost forces ground water upwards.

Surface cracks appear.

Collapsed pingo

Lake

Ice core

Ice core

FIND OUT MORE

ARCTIC OCEAN   CLIMATE   GLACIATION   LAKES   MOUNTAINS AND VALLEYS   SOIL   WEATHER

TUNNELS

HIDDEN AWAY UNDER STREETS, hills, mountains, rivers, and seas are many thousands of kilometres of tunnels. Some carry roads, railways, canals, and pedestrian subways, making transport quicker and safer. Others carry services, such as water supplies, sewage, or communications cables. Using only hand tools, the ancient Greeks and Romans built the first tunnels to supply water to their cities. Modern tunnels are dug by special machines or blasted with explosives. Most tunnels are close to the surface, but mountain tunnels may be hundreds of metres underground.

Cut and cover
The simplest tunnel-building method is cut and cover, which is used for tunnels just below the surface, such as subways. Engineers dig a trench, build the tunnel inside it, and then cover it over.

Building tunnels
The method used to build a tunnel depends on the type of rock (either hard or soft) through which the tunnel will pass, and how deep under the ground the tunnel needs to go. In deep tunnels, the digging takes place at the tunnel face. The waste rock is removed along the tunnel.

Rock blasting
Tunnels are blasted through hard rock by placing high explosives in holes drilled into the rock face. Most hard-rock tunnels are strong enough to support themselves.

Pit props
Narrow tunnels are dug ro reach layers of coal or mineral ore far below the surface. The roof of each tunnel is held up by steel or wooden supports, called pit props.

Conveyor belts move lining segments to the tunnel face.

Concrete tunnel-lining segments

Model of tunnel boring machine (TBM)

Gripper shoes hold rock and thrust TBM forwards.

Control cabin

Rotating head cuts through rock.

Tunnel boring
A tunnel boring machine, or TBM, digs through the soft rock (such as chalk) underneath rivers and seas. The TBM creeps slowly forwards as its spinning cutting-head digs away the rock. The TBM lines the tunnel with concrete as it moves along.

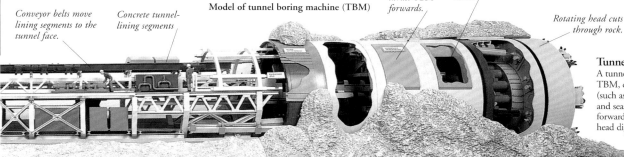

Parts of a tunnel
A tunnel usually consists of a concrete, steel, or brick lining that supports the roof and makes the tunnel waterproof. Many "tunnels" – such as the Channel Tunnel, which runs under the English Channel and links Britain and France – are actually tunnel systems made up of several separate tunnels running parallel with each other. The tunnels are linked by cross passages.

Cross-section of the Channel Tunnel

Fire-fighting equipment

Relief duct stops air pressure building up in tunnels.

Drainage pipes

Communication cables carry train signals, telephone messages, and computer data.

Cooling pipes carry chilled water to absorb heat given off by the trains.

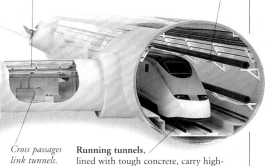

Electricity cables supply power to the trains, and to lighting, signalling, and ventilation equipment.

Service tunnel is used by engineers and emergency services.

Cross passages link tunnels.

Running tunnels, lined with tough concrete, carry high-speed trains travelling in each direction.

Tunnel safety
Modern tunnels are equipped with safety devices to warn of fire, flooding, and other dangers. In the past, miners and tunnel diggers took caged canaries underground. If a canary collapsed, it was a sign that there were poisonous or explosive gases in the air.

Canary

Ventilation
Road and railway tunnels must be well ventilated to provide passengers with fresh air. In long tunnels, particularly where cars emit toxic exhaust gases, there are ventilation shafts leading to the surface, or huge ventilation fans that create a flow of fresh air through the tunnel.

Timeline
1st century AD Roman engineers build an aqueduct that travels through 25 km (19 miles) of tunnels dug with pick axes and shovels.

1818 British engineer Marc Isambard Brunel invents the tunnelling shield – a device that makes underwater tunnelling safer.

Pick axe

1867 Rock tunnelling becomes easier when Swedish chemist Alfred Nobel invents the explosive dynamite.

1871 The Mont Cenis (or Fréjus) tunnel beneath the Alps is the first to be built using compressed-air drills.

1988 Japan's underwater Seikan Tunnel opens – at 54 km (34 miles), it is the world's longest tunnel.

1994 The Channel Tunnel opens between Britain and France.

FIND OUT MORE

BIRDS   BRIDGES   COAL   PRESSURE   ROADS   ROMAN EMPIRE   TRAINS AND RAILWAYS   TRANSPORT, HISTORY OF   WEAPONS

TURKEY

SPLIT BETWEEN Europe and Asia, Turkey has a strategic influence over the Black Sea, Mediterranean, Middle East, and Central Asia, and is divided into two by a huge plateau. The European part has adopted western cultures and boasts steady industry and cosmopolitan cities. Asian Turkey is the country's rustic heartland, steeped in Islamic tradition, and home to farmers and nomads. Following the collapse of the Ottoman Empire in 1913, Turkey underwent a policy of modernization.

Physical features

European Turkey joins the tip of the Balkan Peninsula. In Asian Turkey, coastal plains border the Anatolian plateau, which is enclosed by the Pontic and Taurus Mountain ranges. The mountains converge in a vast region, where the Euphrates and Tigris rivers rise.

TURKEY FACTS

CAPITAL CITY	Ankara
AREA	780,580 sq km (301,382 sq miles)
POPULATION	67,600,000
MAIN LANGUAGE	Turkish
MAJOR RELIGION	Muslim
CURRENCY	Turkish lira
LIFE EXPECTANCY	70 years
PEOPLE PER DOCTOR	833
GOVERNMENT	Multi-party democracy
ADULT LITERACY	85%

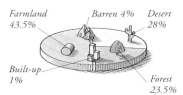

Farmland 43.5% · Barren 4% · Desert 28% · Built-up 1% · Forest 23.5%

Land use

Anatolia's western plateau is used mainly for grazing animals, while the broad, fertile valleys of the Aegean and Mediterranean coasts form the main farming region. About one-third of the land is isolated desert or rocky mountain.

Coastal regions

Turkey is bordered on three sides by long coastlines. The sandy beaches and turquoise seas of the Aegean and Mediterranean coasts give way to fertile plains inland. The unspoilt Black Sea coast also has long, sandy beaches but is more rugged, with mountainous forests and a changeable climate.

Anatolian plateau

Nearly 97 per cent of Turkey is raised, flat-topped land known as Anatolia. The western plateau is dry with few river valleys, while the smaller eastern plateau is rugged, with ochre-red plains, fertile valleys, and rocky caves. Central Anatolia has low mountains and grassy plains.

Lake Van

Turkey's largest lake, Lake Van has an area of 3,736 sq km (1,453 sq miles). It lies in the east of the country near Mount Ararat, and is 1,650 m (5,400 ft) above sea-level.

Tenth-century Armenian church on Akdamar Island, Lake Van

43°C (109°F)   -36°C (-33°F)
23°C (73°F)   0°C (32°F)
367 mm (14 in)

Climate

The Aegean and Mediterranean coastal regions have hot summers and mild winters. The Anatolian plateau and the mountains have mild or warm summers and cold, snowy winters.

Ankara

Purpose-built in central Anatolia on an ancient site, Ankara replaced Istanbul as capital in 1923. The city is dominated by the Mausoleum of Atatürk, the nationalist who liberalized Turkey in the 1920s and 1930s. Giant stone monuments cover more than 1 km (0.6 miles) in area.

Atatürk's Mausoleum

People

Seventy per cent of the people are ethnic Turks. About 20 per cent are Kurds, who live in the extreme east, and there are also Armenians, Arabs, Greeks, and refugees from former Soviet states.

87 per sq km (224 per sq mile)

74% Urban

26% Rural

People
Most Turks live in western Turkey. Many have moved from poor countryside areas to cities to try and make a living on the bustling market stalls, or bazaars. Almost all Turks are united by their shared religion, Islam, which plays a key role in history and culture.

Leisure

Most Turkish leisure pursuits are not considered appropriate for women, though as mothers they may attend family outings. Football and greased wrestling are both popular games for men and draw huge crowds.

Turkish coffee pot

Wrestling
Greased wrestling is the national sport of Turkey. Men smear their bodies with olive oil to resist the grip of their opponents. An annual wrestling feast called *kirkpinar* is held every spring.

Coffee houses
Turkish men meet regularly in coffee houses, or *kiraathanes*, to drink Turkish coffee, which is thick, strong, and sweet. While drinking, men play backgammon and smoke pipes.

Turkish delight – rose- or lemon-flavoured jellies.

Farming

About 38 per cent of Turkey's labour force works in farming. The country's varied climate allows a wide range of crops to be grown. Cotton, which supports a thriving textile industry, and tobacco, grown on the central plateau, are the main export crops.

Sheep and goats
On the pastures of eastern and western Turkey, sheep and goats graze. Goats provide angora wool, named after Turkey's capital, Ankara, originally called Angora.

Rice pilaf

Food
Rice and yoghurt are the base of many Turkish dishes. Lamb or mutton are commonly served, most frequently in a *shish kebab*, in which cubes of meat are grilled on a skewer with onion, peppers, and tomatoes. Fish such as swordfish, shrimps, and mussels, caught off the 8,300 km (5,160 miles) of coastline, are a speciality. *Baklava*, a sweet pastry stuffed with honey and nuts, is a treat.

Roasted pieces of lamb

Yoghurt sauce

Hazelnuts

Figs

Peach

Crops
Turkey is self-sufficient in food, and grows cereals as well as specialized crops such as aubergines, grapes, and dates. Hazelnuts and tea are cultivated along the Black Sea coast. Peaches, melons, and figs, of which Turkey is the world's largest producer, flourish on the warm coasts.

Transport
Bordering the sea on three sides, Turkey has many fine harbours and a merchant fleet of nearly 900 ships. Ferries and two bridges link the Asian and European parts of the country. Turkey also has a railway network, 12,000 km (1,072 miles) in length, which joins its principal cities.

Industry

Turkey has more than 30,000 factories, mainly in the west of the country, which produce processed food, textiles, iron and steel, chemicals, machinery, and vehicles. Mining is concentrated in the east. Turkey has a rapidly expanding tourist industry.

Kilims
Knotted-pile carpets, called *kilims*, are made throughout Turkey. Every year, the country makes about 44,000,000 sq m (474,000,000 sq ft) of carpet. Each region has its own individual designs and colours, and the *kilims* are sold at street markets in every town.

Tourism
More than nine million tourists flock to Turkey every year, attracted by its wealth of historic sites, pleasant climate, and fine beaches. The Aegean coast is dotted with the remains of Greek and Roman cities. Pamukkale, a popular resort since Roman times, draws locals and visitors to its cascading, mineral-rich thermal pools, set on a chalky hillside.

At Pamukkale, calcium deposits form remarkable shapes.

Istanbul

The world's only city to be split between continents, Istanbul lies partly in Europe, partly in Asia. Once called Constantinople, it was Turkey's capital from AD 330–1923. Today, it is Turkey's largest city, home to about 8,000,000 people. It has a mix of colourful bazaars, elaborate mosques, and modern shops.

Sunset over Istanbul

FIND OUT MORE

ASIA, HISTORY OF · COASTS · EUROPE, HISTORY OF · FARMING · ISLAM · OTTOMAN EMPIRE · ROMAN EMPIRE · SEVEN WONDERS OF THE ANCIENT WORLD · SHIPS AND BOATS · TEXTILES AND WEAVING

TURTLES AND TORTOISES

APPROXIMATELY 250 SPECIES of turtle and tortoise exist today. They are reptiles with hard shells and can be found from the tropics to temperate regions. Those that live in water are called turtles; those that live on land are called tortoises. They lack teeth but have sharp horny lip shields. All reproduce by laying eggs, females laying from one to more than 100 eggs in loose soil or sand. Many tortoises and sea turtles are endangered, the result of trade in their shells or meat, and theft of their eggs.

Carapace covers the back.

Plastron covers the belly, and protects against stones and twigs.

Sea turtles

There are seven species of sea turtle. The largest is the leatherback, which grows to 1.8 m (6 ft) long and weighs 680 kg (1,500 lb). Other species include the hawksbill and the loggerhead turtle. Turtles migrate long distances from their feeding grounds to mate near traditional nesting beaches. The females lay up to 160 eggs in pits that they dig in the sand.

Shells

A tortoise or turtle shell comprises many small plate-like bones, and is part of the skeleton. The flat underneath is called the plastron; the domed upper part is called the carapace. The shell is covered by either hard horny plates or leathery skin, and provides protection when the animal withdraws inside.

Tortoises

Most tortoises have stumpy legs and a high rounded upper shell, although the crevice-dwelling pancake tortoise has a flattened upper shell, hence its name. The largest tortoises are the giant Galápagos and Aldabra tortoises of the Pacific and Indian Oceans. Both these species can weigh more than 250 kg (550 lb) and live for more than 150 years.

Hinge-back tortoises

There are three species of hinge-back tortoise, living in Africa and Madagascar. They can close the hind section of their carapace to give added protection to their legs and tail from predators. The plates on this part of the carapace gradually get worn.

Starred tortoise

Adult starred tortoises have a pattern of pale lines radiating over a darker background. This pattern may be indistinguishble on older ones. Young may be entirely yellow with black markings only between the shell plates.

Head, legs, and tail are pulled into shell.

Hinge allows back of shell to bend downwards for added protection.

Swimming

Sea turtles have flipper-like limbs for swimming. They can dive to considerable depths and hold their breath underwater for long periods.

Back pair of flippers used as rudders to steer turtle along.

Turtle shell is streamlined for gliding through water.

Powerful flippers propel the turtle through the water.

 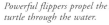 

Green turtle swimming

Head and neck are about 14 cm (5.5 in) long.

Snake-necked turtle

With its long neck, this carnivorous Australasian turtle can snorkel for air from deep water, forage for food in deep holes, and defend any part of its body with a vicious bite. It must turn its head sideways to withdraw it under the carapace.

Freshwater turtles

Sometimes called terrapins, river- and swamp-dwelling turtles are found all over the world. Mostly small, like the 28 cm (11 in) red-eared slider, freshwater turtles also include giant Amazon river turtles, leathery soft-shelled turtles, and snapping turtles such as the 80 cm (31 in) alligator snapping turtle from the southeastern USA.

Legs rather than flippers allow the turtle to walk on land.

Turtles have a flatter carapace than tortoises.

Leopard tortoise hatching

1 The hatchling tortoise begins to crack the egg with a projection on its lip.

2 The egg shell fragments as the baby tortoise moves around inside.

3 The hatchling learns to use its lungs to breathe for the first time.

4 When the yolk has been absorbed, the hatchling leaves the egg.

STARRED TORTOISE

SCIENTIFIC NAME	*Geochelene elegans*
ORDER	Testudines
FAMILY	Testudinidae
DISTRIBUTION	Central and southern India and Sri Lanka
HABITAT	Dry and wet forests
DIET	Vegetation
SIZE	Length 25 cm (10 in)

FIND OUT MORE CONSERVATION EGGS MARSH AND SWAMP WILDLIFE MIGRATION, ANIMAL OCEAN WILDLIFE REPTILES

Tortoises

Starred tortoise from India and Sri Lanka has a star pattern on its carapace.

Leopard tortoise is from dry parts of Africa. It has a spotted pattern.

Red-legged tortoise from South America has large red scales on its front legs.

Characteristic red scales

Stumpy front feet with short toes for walking

Hinged rear section of carapace

Hinge-back tortoise from Africa has a flexible section of carapace that hinges downwards to protect its rear quarters.

Herman's tortoise lives in areas in south and southeastern Europe where summers are hot. It hibernates in winter.

Pattern of radiating lines

Radiated tortoise from Madagascar has been known to live for at least 137 years.

Turtles

Red stripe easily identifies this species.

Yellow-bellied slider is a close relative of the red-eared slider. This one is a newly hatched juvenile.

Leathery carapace lacks the characteristic hard scutes of other turtles.

Male red-eared sliders have long front toenails, used in courting females.

Red-eared slider of North America is commonly kept as a pet.

Spiny soft-shelled turtle lies buried in the sand of lake- or riverbeds in North America, ready to ambush passing prey.

Large head with a strong beak cannot be retracted fully into the shell.

Shell colour is often hidden by growths of algae.

Mississippi mud turtle is known as a sawback when young because of the ridge down its shell.

Common snapping turtle is a voracious American turtle with a powerful bite.

Big-headed turtle from Southeast Asia is a poor swimmer, but a good climber.

Painted turtle has a brightly patterned carapace.

Neck as long as or longer than the body

Smooth, dark-coloured carapace

Snake-necked turtle from Australia actively hunts for aquatic animals. It sleeps with its long neck tucked sideways under the carapace.

Shell is used for tortoiseshell products.

White-lipped mud turtle has a double-hinged plastron that allows it to close up like a box.

European pond terrapin is the most widespread European turtle.

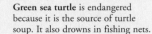

Big-headed mud turtle has a large head and powerful jaws. It is known locally in Belize as "toe-biter".

Green sea turtle is endangered because it is the source of turtle soup. It also drowns in fishing nets.

Alligator snapping turtle is the largest American freshwater turtle.

Razor-sharp lips

TWAIN, MARK

MILLIONS OF READERS, young and old, have enjoyed *The Adventures of Huckleberry Finn*, the story of an unconventional boy and a runaway slave as they travel down the Mississippi River on a raft. But behind the book is the amazing story of its author, Mark Twain. Born in 1835, Twain lost his father when he was 12. He worked as a printer, publisher, and river-boat pilot, using his experiences of life on the mid-west frontier of the USA in a series of books that changed American literature through their humour and use of everyday speech.

Samuel Clemens

Mark Twain was born Samuel Langhorne Clemens in 1835 in Missouri, mid-western USA. After the death of his father in 1847, Clemens was apprenticed to a printer in Hannibal, on the banks of the Mississippi River. Here he began his writing career, working on a newspaper owned by his brother.

Lecturer

When the American Civil War broke out in 1861, most traffic on the river stopped and Twain lost his job. He began writing for the *Virginia City Examiner* and later joined a newspaper in San Francisco. He began to publish humorous stories under the name Mark Twain and travelled widely, lecturing about his exploits to appreciative audiences.

Innocents abroad

After his return from a trip to the Mediterranean and Holy Land in 1869, Twain wrote of his journey in a book, *The Innocents Abroad*. The success of the book established Twain as an author, as well as beginning an American literary obsession with the "Old World".

Mississippi steamer

Steamboat pilot

In 1857, Clemens travelled south to New Orleans to seek his fortune in South America. But he never left the city, becoming instead a river-boat pilot on the Mississippi. While working on the river, he adopted the pseudonym Mark Twain. "Mark Twain" is the pilot's call, marking two fathoms' depth of water. Many of the sights he saw and people he met in his journeys along the river appear in Twain's later novels and short stories.

Clemens' pilot's licence

Charles Webster and Co

In the 1870s, Twain set up his own publishing company to print and publish his own novels and stories. He wrote a stream of books, including *A Tramp Abroad* (1880), inspired by a walking tour in Germany; *The Prince and the Pauper* (1882), a historical fantasy set in England; and *Life on the Mississippi* (1883), an autobiography of Twain's time as a river-boat pilot. By this time, Twain had become one of America's most celebrated authors.

Connecticut Yankee

Twain's *A Connecticut Yankee in King Arthur's Court*, published in 1889, is a disturbing satire, mixing historical and present-day characters. Twain contrasts the common sense of the American character with the superstition of the British court, to say something about the vast differences between the societies.

The Connecticut Yankee

Tom Sawyer and Huckleberry Finn

Two books by Twain have made him one of the best-loved authors of all time – *The Adventures of Tom Sawyer* (1876) and its sequel, *The Adventures of Huckleberry Finn* (1885). Both books draw on Twain's childhood in Hannibal, and paint an unforgettable picture of frontier life on the Mississippi River. Although full of humour, both of these books make profound moral comments on American life, in particular, the institution of slavery.

Bankruptcy

In 1894, most of Twain's business ventures had failed and he was deeply in debt. To pay off his debts, he embarked on lengthy lecture tours and wrote books and stories designed to cash in on his famous name.

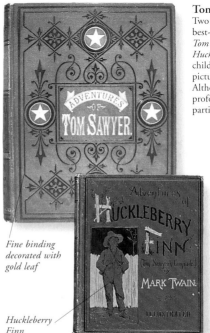

Fine binding decorated with gold leaf

Huckleberry Finn

Later life

In his later years, Twain toured the world giving lectures. He was awarded honorary degrees by universities all over the world, including Oxford, England. His last years were marked by tragedy. By 1904, two of his three daughters had died, followed, after a lengthy illness, by his wife. In 1906, his own death was reported while he was still alive, forcing him to cable the Associated Press agency stating that "the report of my death was an exaggeration".

Twain's Oxford gown

MARK TWAIN

1835	Born in Florida, Missouri.
1857–61	Works as river-boat pilot.
1867	*The Celebrated Jumping Frog of Calaveras County*, a collection of short stories and sketches.
1869	*The Innocents Abroad*
1876	*The Adventures of Tom Sawyer*
1883	*Life on the Mississippi*
1885	*The Adventures of Huckleberry Finn*
1895–96	Series of lecture tours.
1910	Dies in Connecticut.

FIND OUT MORE BOOKS LITERATURE UNITED STATES, HISTORY OF WRITING

UNIONS, TRADE

AROUND THE WORLD, the response of working people to poor conditions or low pay has been to organize themselves into trade unions. Trade unions are formed and run by their members to represent their interests, and may sometimes conflict with employers or governments. In Britain, Australia, and the USA, unions are organized by craft, with unions of miners and engineers, while in the rest of Europe they are organized by industry, with unions of workers in the car or chemical industries.

Tolpuddle Martyrs
In 1834, six English farm workers from the village of Tolpuddle in Dorset, England, were deported to Australia for seven years for daring to organize a trade union. After a big campaign, they were pardoned in 1836.

Inside trade unions

A trade union is run by and for its members. The members elect the leading officers, who run the union's administration, and meet regularly to decide union policy and debate issues of common concern. Because of their large size, most unions are organized on a local factory or workplace basis, co-ordinated regionally and nationally.

Membership papers

Membership badges

Membership
Traditionally, trade unions have recruited male manual, or "blue-collar", workers. Today, many clerical and professional people, known as "white-collar" workers, as well as many more women, are union members. White-collar workers include civil servants, teachers, and journalists.

Workers in a car factory in Germany, where trade unions are organized by industry.

Services
Trade unions offer a wide range of services to their members, in addition to their work of negotiating employment conditions. Banking, insurance, pensions, credit cards, loans, and many other financial and personal services are all provided to support existing members and to encourage new members to join.

International unionism

Two international organizations exist to support trade unions around the world: the Communist-led World Federation of Trade Unions, set up in 1945, and the International Confederation of Free Trade Unions, established in 1949.

What unions do

Trade unions exist to support their members at work. They campaign for better pay and improved conditions, negotiate pay rises and other benefits, and represent individual members at tribunals and on health and safety issues.

Hard hat

Ear protectors

Strike
The ultimate weapon of any trade union is to call its members out on strike – that is, to refuse to work. Although strikes can be an effective weapon in achieving what unions want for their members, they can cause considerable hardship as workers lose their pay and possibly their jobs.

Collective bargaining
Trade unions bargain with the management to improve their members' working conditions. The two sides negotiate until they reach a deal that gives them both what they want. Without a trade union, individual workers must do this for themselves.

Industrial boards
In Sweden and some other European countries, trade unions sit on the management boards of companies and work with government and employers to help tackle national industrial and economic problems.

Lech Walesa
The Polish trade unionist Lech Walesa (b. 1943) was sacked from the Gdansk shipyards in 1976 for leading a strike. Walesa then set up a trade union called Solidarity, in opposition to the government. It was formally recognized in 1980. After Communism's fall, he became President of Poland in 1990.

Timeline

Early 1800s Industrial Revolution and the growth of factories leads to the formation of the first trade unions in Europe and the USA.

1850s Trade unions are formed in most European countries.

1868 First meeting of the Trades Union Congress (TUC) held in Manchester, UK.

1881 American Federation of Labor (AFL) set up.

1919 International Labour Organization (ILO) set up and affiliated to the League of Nations.

1926 General Strike causes state of paralysis in Britain.

1946 ILO affiliates with the UN, to improve workers' conditions through international agreement.

1955 AFL merges with the more militant Congress of Industrial Organizations (CIO).

FIND OUT MORE   EUROPE, HISTORY OF   GOVERNMENTS AND POLITICS   INDUSTRIAL REVOLUTION   MONEY   TRADE AND INDUSTRY   UNITED NATIONS

UNITED KINGDOM

THE UNITED KINGDOM consists of England, Wales, and Scotland, which make up the island of Great Britain, Northern Ireland, and hundreds of smaller islands. Great Britain is separated from mainland Europe by the English Channel and the North Sea. Highly urbanized and densely populated, the UK is one of the world's leading industrial economies and one of its oldest monarchies. The Isle of Man and the Channel Islands are self-governing Crown dependencies: the UK government handles their international affairs.

UNITED KINGDOM FACTS

CAPITAL CITY London

AREA 244,820 sq km (94,525 sq miles)

POPULATION 59,500,000

MAIN LANGUAGE English

MAJOR RELIGIONS Christian, Muslim, Hindu, Sikh, Jewish

CURRENCY Pound sterling

LIFE EXPECTANCY 78 years

PEOPLE PER DOCTOR 556

GOVERNMENT Multi-party democracy

ADULT LITERACY 99%

Physical features

The rolling green fields of southern England contrast with the flat, marshy Fens in the east. Scotland, Wales, and northern England have craggy mountains and windswept moors and fells. Northern Ireland has undulating pasture and low coastal mountains.

Coastline

The UK has more than 5,000 km (3,000 miles) of coast. The rocky inlets and cliffs of the Cornish coast in southwest England contrast with the broad, sandy beaches in the southeast. The English Channel coast is characterized by the distinctive chalky "white cliffs of Dover".

Countryside

Viewed from the air, the English countryside forms a neat patchwork of colour that reflects generations of farming and cultivation. The pattern is broken only by farms, villages, and country roads. Fields are traditionally separated by hedgerows, many of which mark ancient boundaries. The hedges also provide a valuable refuge for wildlife.

Climate

The UK has a generally mild climate, but the weather is changeable. Rainfall is highest in the north and west, and lowest in the extreme southeast. Winter snow is common in northern and mountainous areas.

34°C (93°F)   -17°C (1°F)
18°C (64°F)   5°C (41°F)

600 mm (24 in)

Farmland 71%   Barren 4%

Land use

More than two-thirds of the UK is used for cultivating crops and rearing livestock. The most built-up region is southeast England. Scotland is five times less densely populated than the rest of the UK.

Built-up 11%   Forest 14%

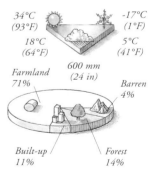

London

Capital of the UK, the largest city in Europe and home to about seven million people, London is the hub of British business and government. Founded by the Romans as a centre for trade with the rest of Europe, London is an exciting, bustling city. Every year, thousands of tourists visit its historic buildings, museums, galleries, and shops, and ride on traditional double-decker buses.

Big Ben and the House of Commons

U

People

The English, Scottish, Welsh, and Irish each have their own customs, traditions, and even languages. British society is still divided by a class system based on heredity and wealth. The standard of living is good, but poverty exists in some inner-city areas.

89%
Urban

11%
Rural

240 per sq km
(622 per sq mile)

Multicultural society
Since the 1950s, thousands of people have settled in the UK from former colonies in Asia, Africa, and the Caribbean. The result is a multicultural society with a wide range of food, art, music, religions, and festivals, such as London's colourful Notting Hill Carnival.

Leisure

The British are great sports fans and enjoy playing and watching soccer, rugby, cricket, golf, snooker, and tennis. Fishing, walking, and cycling are popular outdoor pursuits. Many people, however, prefer to go to the theatre or cinema, or relax at home with the TV or a good newspaper.

Gardening
The British are avid gardeners and spend many hours out of doors creating colourful seasonal displays. Thousands of people flock to flower shows and open days, and garden centres selling a variety of plants, books, and equipment are big business.

Cricket
A summer cricket match on the village green is a traditional English scene. The English invented the game in the 1300s, and it is now played in many counties.

Farming

British farming is highly mechanized and produces 66 per cent of the UK's food, but only one per cent of the labour force works on the land. Most farms are small and are often run on a part-time basis, employing only one or two workers. Farming of both animals and crops is common.

Dartmoor sheep

Hereford bull

Crops
Wheat, barley, sugar beet, and potatoes are Britain's most widely grown crops. Kent, in the southeast, is famous for its hops for making beer. Large farms in eastern England produce cereals and vegetables such as peas and beans.

Livestock
Beef and dairy cattle are reared in areas of lush pasture. Sheep are reared in hilly, more rugged areas. Chicken and pigs are raised intensively in sheds, as well as free-range in the open.

Food

The British are best known for their cooked breakfasts, roast dinners, and afternoon teas. Fast food and takeaways probably started here, with fish and chips, the sandwich – a British invention – and Cornish pasties. The UK also produces a wide range of cheeses such as Cheddar and Stilton. The national drinks are tea, beer, and Scotch whisky.

A typical cooked English breakfast

Industry

Until recently, Britain had thriving coal, iron, and steel industries. Today, oil and natural gas from the North Sea have replaced coal, and light engineering and financial and service industries have become the mainstay of the economy. Reduced fish stocks have caused a decline in the fishing industry.

Banking
Dominated by glossy office buildings such as the Lloyds Building, the City of London is one of the world's leading financial centres. Situated strategically between Tokyo and New York City, more currency changes hands here than in any other city.

The Lloyds Building by Sir Richard Rogers

Cars
Britain ranks highly in world car production and produces about 1,300,000 vehicles a year. The industry has attracted investment from US, German, and Japanese manufacturers. Vehicles make up ten per cent of exports. Famous makes include Rolls Royce, Vauxhall, and Rover.

Tourism
More than 25 million tourists visit Britain every year. Many are drawn by the history and culture of cities such as London and Edinburgh, while others are attracted by the wild scenery of Scotland, Wales, and the Lake District.

Transport

Large container lorries transport nearly all Britain's freight over an extensive network of roads and motorways. The British drive on the left. Intercity trains are generally fast, comfortable, and efficient. Britain is also an international gateway for air and sea traffic.

Channel Tunnel
The Channel Tunnel, Britain's first rail link with continental Europe, opened in 1994. High-speed Eurostar trains make the journey from London to Paris and Brussels in three hours. The tunnel is 50 km (31 miles) long, and 75 per cent runs under the sea.

Heathrow Airport
Situated within easy reach of the city, Heathrow is the largest of London's airports. It handles about 62,000,000 passengers and 480,000 flights annually. Plans for a new terminal, the fifth, are under way.

FIND OUT MORE — AIRPORTS · BALL GAMES · EMPIRES · EUROPE, HISTORY OF · EUROPEAN UNION · FARMING · FESTIVALS · GARDENS · MONEY · TUNNELS · UNITED KINGDOM, HISTORY OF

UNITED KINGDOM, HISTORY OF

THROUGHOUT THEIR HISTORY, the British Isles have been subject to frequent invasions. In turn, Celts, Romans, Anglo-Saxons, and Vikings invaded the islands and established their rule. In 1066, the Normans invaded and subjugated England. Thereafter, England emerged as the strongest nation, conquering first Ireland, and then Wales, before joining with Scotland in 1603. The United Kingdom thus formed the leading industrial and colonial power in the world, maintaining a supremacy that was to last into the present century.

Ancient British harness mount

Ancient Britain
The earliest inhabitants of Britain were nomadic hunter-gatherers, who moved from place to place in search of food. In about 4000 BC, people began to settle in villages, farm the land, and raise animals.

Roman Britain

Julius Caesar invaded Britain in 54 BC to stop local Celtic tribes helping the Gauls in France to undermine the Roman Empire. In AD 43, England and Wales were conquered and made part of the empire. The Romans built many towns and roads, and encouraged trade.

Roman towns
The Romans built a network of towns as centres of trade and local government. Among these were Londinium (London) on the River Thames, and Aquae Sulis (Bath) in the west of England.

Roman baths in the city of Bath

Anglo-Saxon invasions

After the Romans left in 410, Germanic Anglo-Saxons from northern Europe began to invade Britain. By 613, the Anglo-Saxons had conquered all of England, dividing it into seven kingdoms.

Christ is offered a sponge soaked in vinegar, to quench his thirst.

Anglo-Saxon relief of the crucifixion, Daglingworth, England

St Augustine
Under Roman rule, most of Britain was Christian, but the Anglo-Saxons had their own gods. Christian missionary St Augustine came to Canterbury in 597 and began to convert the area to Christianity.

Vikings and Cnut
In 787, Viking sailors made their first raid on the English coast, and soon controlled the north and east of the country. In 1013, they seized the entire kingdom; under King Cnut, England was part of a Viking empire called the Danelaw that included much of Scandinavia.

King Cnut

Norman England

In 1066, William Duke of Normandy invaded England to claim the throne. Near Hastings, he defeated the English army led by King Harold, and conquered the country. The Normans built castles to enforce their rule, and provided England with strong central government.

Bayeaux tapestry, showing the Norman victory

Magna Carta
Under Norman rule, arguments frequently occurred between the king and his most powerful lords. In 1215, at Runnymede in Surrey, King John signed the Magna Carta, a document drawn up by senior lords. It laid down the responsibilities and rights of citizens and the Church in relation to the crown. The Magna Carta is still one of the major constitutional documents of English government.

Magna Carta

Royal seal of King John

William I
William I (c.1027–87) was a descendant of Vikings who had settled in Normandy in northern France. As king of England, he was a strong ruler who brought stability to the country. He died after falling from his horse at Nantes, France.

Parliament
In 1265, Henry III called representatives of the towns, lords, and clergy, to the first parliament in London to advise the government. Within a century, parliament had the right to make laws and levy taxes.

Modern Houses of Parliament

Wales
England tried to rule Wales from Saxon times, but the Welsh princes resisted. In 1282, Edward I conquered the country, and built many castles to keep the Welsh subdued. An Act of Union in 1536 formally joined Wales to England. The Welsh language was suppressed for centuries afterwards.

Dolbadarn Castle, Wales

Tudors and Stuarts

Henry VII, the first Tudor king, seized power in 1485. He curbed the power of the lords, restored royal finances, and ruled strongly. The Tudors ruled until 1603. They were followed by the Stuarts, under whom England tried to keep its leading role in Europe, in spite of a bitter civil war.

Dissolution of the monasteries
In 1534, Henry VIII broke with the Roman Catholic Church because it refused to grant him a divorce. He created the Church of England, with him as its supreme head, dissolved the monasteries to get money for his court, and seized Church lands.

Henry VIII, the second Tudor king, painted by Hans Holbein

Royalist officer's coat

Parliamentarian backplate

Royalist helmet

Royalist buff coat

Royalist armour

Royalist backplate

Parliamentarian breastplate

Parliamentarian soldier's hat

English Civil War
Conflicts between parliament and Charles I over the government of the country broke out into open war in 1642. The king was defeated and was executed in 1649. England became a republic until 1660.

Scotland
Scotland first became a kingdom in 843, and remained independent for centuries despite constant invasions by England. In 1603, the Scottish king, James VI, inherited the English throne from the Tudor queen Elizabeth I; in 1707, the two countries were formally united.

Crown of Scotland

Industrial England

In the 18th century, Britain became the world's first industrialized country. Millions of people moved from the countryside to the towns to work in new factories and workshops. Canals and railways moved raw materials and finished goods around the country. By 1850, Britain was the "workshop of the world".

Victorian England
During the reign of Queen Victoria (1837–1901), Britain became the world's richest country, with an empire that covered one-quarter of the globe. Despite this wealth, living conditions were poor for many people in the cities.

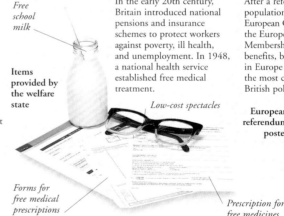

Crystal Palace, site of the Great Exhibition of 1851

Chartist demonstration

Chartists
In the early 19th century, demands grew for better representation of working people in government. In the 1830s and 1840s, groups such as the Chartists campaigned for reform. They were named after the People's Charter, drafted by William Lovett in 1838. Reforms were only granted much later.

Modern Britain

During the 20th century, Britain underwent many changes. It granted much of its empire independence, lost control of most of Ireland, and struggled to cope with economic decline. In the late 20th century, Britain became a more multi-cultural society, as many immigrants arrived from the country's former colonies in Africa, Asia, and the Caribbean.

Wartime Britain
In 1940, Britain stood alone in the fight against Nazi Germany. British fighter pilots fought off a planned German invasion during the Battle of Britain, but British cities were heavily bombed throughout World War II.

Londoners shelter in the underground during air raids.

Free school milk

Items provided by the welfare state

Welfare state
In the early 20th century, Britain introduced national pensions and insurance schemes to protect workers against poverty, ill health, and unemployment. In 1948, a national health service established free medical treatment.

Low-cost spectacles

Forms for free medical prescriptions

Prescription for free medicines

Entry into Europe
After a referendum of the adult population, Britain joined the European Community (now called the European Union) in 1973. Membership brought many benefits, but the role of Britain in Europe has remained one of the most controversial issues for British political parties.

European referendum poster

Timeline

FIND OUT MORE   ANGLO-SAXONS   ELIZABETH I   EMPIRES   EUROPE, HISTORY OF   EUROPEAN UNION   INDUSTRIAL REVOLUTION   IRELAND, HISTORY OF   VIKINGS   WORLD WAR I   WORLD WAR II

U

UNITED NATIONS

AT THE HEIGHT OF WORLD WAR II, the 26 Allied countries fighting Germany, Italy, and Japan, pledged as the "United Nations" not to make a separate peace with the enemy. From this declaration grew the UN, a new international organization that aimed to keep world peace and bring warring nations closer together. Today, the UN includes almost every state in the world as a member. Its main success has been to act as an international forum where issues can be discussed and often resolved.

The League of Nations
Set up in 1919 after World War I, the League of Nations was designed to preserve peace and settle disputes by arbitration. However, the League had no armies of its own to enforce its decisions and relied instead on sanctions against offending nations. The absence of the USA and other important nations weakened the League, which collapsed during World War II. It was replaced by the UN.

General Assembly

The main forum in the UN is the General Assembly. Every member state sends one delegate to the Assembly, which meets for four months a year. Decisions are made by a simple majority vote, unless they are so important that they require a two-thirds majority. The Assembly has few powers, but it does serve as an international parliament in which member states can discuss issues of mutual concern.

Secretariat building, where the daily administration is carried out.

Flags of member nations fly in front of the UN complex.

International Court of Justice
International legal disputes between nations are settled at the International Court at The Hague in the Netherlands. The court consists of 15 judges elected by the Security Council and the General Assembly and makes its decisions by a majority vote.

Visitors' entrance

The UN headquarters is in New York, USA. This site is an international zone and has its own stamps and post office.

The Conference Building houses meeting rooms for several UN councils.

Security Council

The Trusteeship Council is responsible for trust territories placed under its supervision by member states.

Economic and Social Council

Peace garden has 25 varieties of rose.

Security Council
The most powerful part of the UN is the Security Council. The council has a membership of 15, comprising five permanent members – USA, Russia, China, UK, and France – and 10 members elected for two-year terms by the General Assembly. The Council can meet at any time and can call on the armies of member states to enforce its decisions.

Economic and Social Council
The 54 members of the Economic and Social Council monitor the economic, social, cultural, health, and educational affairs of member states and work to ensure human rights throughout the world. The Council reports to the General Assembly.

Peacekeeping statue outside UN headquarters

Let Us Beat Swords Into Plowshares

Secretariat
The day-to-day administration of the UN is in the hands of the Secretariat. The staff of the Secretariat comes from every nation and works both in the headquarters of the UN in New York and in any country in the world where the UN is active.

Secretary-General
The most powerful person in the UN is the Secretary-General, who is elected for a five-year term by the General Assembly. Boutros Boutros-Ghali (b. 1922), shown here, was UN Secretary-General from 1992–96. As Secretary-General, he mediated in international disputes, and played a role in international diplomacy. However, the Secretary-General can only act if the Security Council members reach a joint agreement on policy.

Specialized agencies

Much of the detailed work of the UN is carried out by 15 specialized agencies affiliated with the UN. Some of the agencies, such as the International Labour Organization (ILO), were set up before the UN was founded; others are more recent. The organizations cover such areas as international aviation control, trade union and labour affairs, maritime law, and aid and development.

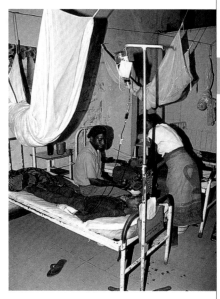

UNICEF
The United Nations Children's Emergency Fund (UNICEF) works for children around the world. It provides health care and health education in many developing countries and plays a vital role in looking after children orphaned or injured by war.

UNESCO
The United Nations Educational, Scientific, and Cultural Organization (UNESCO) was set up in 1946 to promote international cultural collaboration. Its broad range of activities includes restoring sites of cultural value, such as the Angkor Wat temple in Cambodia.

IMF
The International Monetary Fund (IMF) was set up in 1944 to promote international monetary co-operation and stability, and the expansion of world trade. The IMF advises member nations on their economic and financial policies.

WHO
The World Health Organization (WHO) works to improve standards of health and combat disease. Its most important achievement was the complete eradication of smallpox from the world by 1980. Other successful campaigns have been waged against polio and leprosy.

The work of the UN

The UN and its agencies are active in almost every country of the world, paying most attention to the poorer, less-developed nations and to areas of the world affected by war, civil strife, drought, or famine. The UN can offer its own technical assistance and advice, but relies on the support of member nations to provide the necessary funds, personnel, and, in case of war, army troops.

Peacekeeping sculpture outside UN headquarters

Peacekeeping
The UN tries to keep the peace between warring nations or sides in a civil war. The famous blue berets of UN troops have been in operation in most of the world's trouble spots, including the Middle East and former Yugoslavia. At the start of 2002, UN peacekeeping missions operated in 15 nations, deploying 47,000 troops.

Humanitarian aid
The UN plays an important role in providing humanitarian aid to people in distress. The UN High Commissioner for Refugees, based in Geneva, Switzerland, provides food and shelter for refugees fleeing war, famine, or drought, while other UN agencies work to improve water supplies or local health and education provision.

Environmental role
The UN has taken a major role in environmental issues as concern rises about threats to the world's ecology. In 1992, it convened a major conference in Rio de Janeiro, Brazil, on the environment and development. The conference, known as the Earth Summit, committed world nations to reduce pollution in order to prevent global warming.

A UN conference in 1996 votes to ban all nuclear testing.

Dag Hammarskjöld
The Swedish politician Dag Hammarskjöld (1905–61) became UN Secretary-General in 1953. He was a skilled diplomat who raised the prestige of the UN through his impartial handling of international crises, such as the invasion of Suez in 1956. In 1961, Hammarskjöld was killed in a plane crash. He was awarded the 1961 Nobel Peace Prize after his death.

Timeline
1945 San Francisco Conference drafts the UN Charter, which is ratified at the first meeting of the UN in London in October.

1946 Trygve Lie of Norway becomes the first UN Secretary-General.

Permanent members of the Security Council

1950–53 UN sends troops to South Korea to repel invasion by North Korea.

1953 Dag Hammarskjöld becomes Secretary-General.

1960–64 UN intervenes in civil war in the Congo (Zaïre).

1961 U Thant from Burma becomes Secretary-General.

1964 UN sends troops to keep the peace in Cyprus.

1971 Taiwan expelled from UN and its place taken by China.

1972 Kurt Waldheim of Austria becomes Secretary-General.

1982 Javier Pérez de Cuéllar of Peru becomes Secretary-General.

1992 UN troops are deployed in Bosnia after civil war erupts in the states of the former Yugoslavia.

1992 Boutros Boutros-Ghali of Egypt becomes Secretary-General.

1997 Kofi Annan of Ghana becomes Secretary-General.

 FIND OUT MORE ARMIES   COLD WAR   ECOLOGY AND ECOSYSTEMS   EUROPE, HISTORY OF   GOVERNMENTS AND POLITICS   MEDICINE   MONEY   PEACE MOVEMENTS   POLLUTION   WARFARE

UNITED STATES OF AMERICA

THE WORLD'S WEALTHIEST COUNTRY, the United States of America (USA) is also the fourth largest and the third most populated. It is made up of 50 states, 48 of which occupy the central part of North America. Alaska, the 49th state, lies in the northwest of North America and Hawaii, the 50th state, is a chain of Pacific islands. The USA is a major industrial and economic force; since 1945, it has also played a leading role in world affairs.

UNITED STATES OF AMERICA FACTS

CAPITAL CITY	Washington DC
AREA	9,626,091 sq km (3,717,792 sq miles)
POPULATION	281,400,000
MAIN LANGUAGES	English, Spanish
MAJOR RELIGION	Christian
CURRENCY	US dollar
LIFE EXPECTANCY	77 years
PEOPLE PER DOCTOR	370
GOVERNMENT	Multi-party democracy
ADULT LITERACY	99%

Physical features

A vast flat plain lies between the high Rocky Mountains in the west and the weathered Appalachians of eastern USA. The Mississippi River flows south across the plain. Thick forests grow in the northwest.

57°C (135°F) 25°C (77°F) -62°C (-80°F) 1°C (34°F)
1,064 mm (42 in)

Climate
Summers are hot and humid; subtropical in Florida and tropical in Hawaii. Winters are snowy, and notably bitter in Alaska and the mountains. Storms, hurricanes, floods, and droughts are frequent.

Monument Valley
In the arid desert of Arizona is Monument Valley, where giant rocks up to 300 m (1,000 ft) have eroded from red sandstone. The Mittens, so-called because they look like hands, are a striking feature.

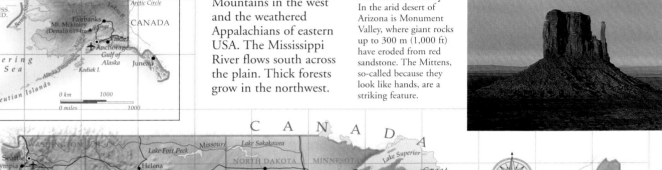

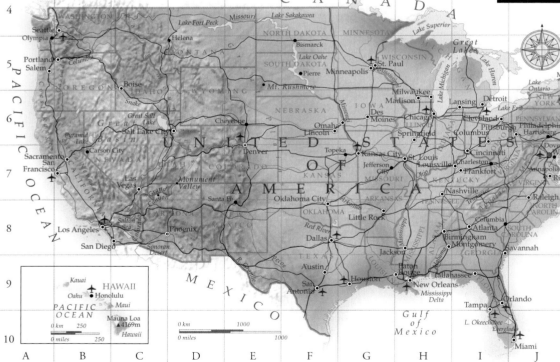

Washington DC
Named after the first US president, the capital, Washington, lies between Virginia and Maryland. Home to 572,000, it is the centre of government and has many green parks and majestic marble buildings.

The Capitol Building

Built-up 0.5%   Forest 37.5%   Wetland 2.5%
Barren 3.5%
Farmland 29.5%   Grassland 9.5%   Tundra 5%   Desert 12%

Land use
The USA has huge forests, which serve a large timber and wood-pulp industry. On the vast fertile plains, or prairies, farmers cultivate wheat and half of the world's maize.

31 per sq km (80 per sq mile)

People
The USA has a diverse, multiracial population. Throughout its history, waves of immigrants have arrived from Europe, Africa, Asia, and South America.

77% Urban   23% Rural

Northeastern states

One of the first regions to be settled by European immigrants, the northeastern states have a rich historical and cultural heritage, and are a melting pot of peoples and cultures. Thanks to rich mineral resources, and many good harbours and rivers, this area has become the most industrialized and heavily populated part of the USA. Busy cities, such as Boston, New York City, Pittsburgh, and Philadelphia, contrast with the unspoiled rural farmsteads of New England.

New York City
Covering an area of 780 sq km (301 sq miles), New York City is the largest city in the USA and a leader in the arts, business, and finance. Wall Street's Stock Exchange is the world's biggest, while Broadway is the heart of theatre land. More than 19 million people live and work in the New York metropolitan area, which stretches into New Jersey and Connecticut, enjoying its rich social and cultural mix and vibrant customs and festivals.

At the end of October, city markets sell giant pumpkins for Halloween.

Fishing
The North Atlantic coastal waters are rich in fish such as cod, herring, and clams. Maine alone has 3,840 km (2400 miles) of coast, and the state is famous for its lobsters.

Tourism
More than 50 million people visit the USA every year, and many come to the northeastern states, attracted by the rolling countryside and rich autumn colours of New England, as the maple leaves turn bright red and gold. Tourists flock to New York City and Niagara Falls, on the border with Canada. Fishing, rafting, hiking, and skiing are popular in this region.

Newspapers
More than 1,700 daily and 7,500 weekly newspapers are produced in the USA. Most newpapers are local, with the exception of the *Wall Street Journal*, which has a national circulation of 2,200,000, *USA Today*, which covers the diversity of life across the USA, and the *New York Times*. The newsprint media is facing increasing competition from satellite and cable television and the Internet.

Cranberry farming
On meticulously cultivated water fields, cranberries are grown in large quantities. The scarlet berries are made into a sauce that is served with turkey at Thanksgiving, juiced, or used as a filling in pancakes.

Great Lakes states

The six states of Minnesota, Wisconsin, Illinois, Indiana, Michigan, and Ohio lie on the shores of the Great Lakes. Ocean ships serve lake ports, which are linked to the Mississippi River, whose trade routes to the Gulf of Mexico have boosted the region's agricultural and manufacturing industries. Vast natural resources, such as coal, iron, copper, and wood, and the fertile land of the prairies have brought this area much prosperity.

Motown records

Motown records
The USA has produced some of the most important popular music forms. In 1959, record producer Berry Gordy founded the Tamla Motown record label in Detroit, known as the "Motor Town". He promoted many black singers, including Stevie Wonder and Diana Ross.

Hamburgers
The USA is a giant in the production and consumption of fast food – 200 burgers are eaten every second in the USA. The hamburger originated in Hamburg, Germany and was brought across the Atlantic by German immigrants. Now, burgers are enjoyed worldwide.

Hamburger

Sears Tower, world's second tallest habitable building

Chicago has 43 km (27 miles) of beaches.

Car industry
Detroit is the centre of the USA's car industry and, together, General Motors, Chrysler, and Ford employ about ten per cent of the city's work-force. More than five million cars are produced annually.

Chicago
America's third largest city, with a population of 2,900,000, Chicago is often called the "Windy City" because of the breezes that sweep in from Lake Michigan. Chicago is a centre of bold architectural innovation and a city of competing skyscrapers. The 110-storey Sears Tower, rising to 520 m (1,707 ft), was built in 1973.

Sailing
The five Great Lakes of North America form the world's largest area of fresh water, and attract millions of visitors each year. Marinas line their shores, and behind them are hundreds of holiday homes.

Central and mountain states

The ten central and mountain states run from Montana, on the Canadian border, down to Oklahoma in the south. In this region of contrasts, the vast, open fields of the Great Plains, watered by the Mississippi and its tributaries, meet the steep Rocky Mountains. Tornadoes are common in the spring. Most of the people who live here are employed in the booming farming and mining industries.

Yellowstone National Park
Opened in 1872, Yellowstone, in northern Wyoming, was the first American national park. Covering 8,991 sq km (3,471 sq miles), the park's natural habitat is home to black and grizzly bears, and many species of animal and bird. It has hot springs and more than 200 geysers, including Old Faithful, which erupts, on average, every 73 minutes.

Cereals
The large farms of the Midwest are highly mechanized and efficient. Iowa is often called "the corn state", because it grows 20 per cent of America's maize, and its cereal factory at Cedar Rapids is the world's largest.

Cowboys
Modern American cowboys tend beef cattle on luxury family-run ranches on the plains. Increasingly, they are abandoning their traditional horseback lifestyle and keeping watch on the herd with the use of helicopters and pick-up trucks.

Traditional high-crowned Stetson

Western saddle

Carved heads of presidents Washington, Lincoln, Jefferson, and Roosevelt

Mount Rushmore
It took more than 14 years to create the faces of four US presidents in the granite cliffs of Mount Rushmore, South Dakota. Carved by Gutzon Borglum, whose son finished them in 1941, the heads stand 18 m (60 ft) tall and attract thousands of tourists.

Gold
Since gold was discovered in South Dakota in 1874, its Homestake Mine, the USA's largest, has been one of the world's main gold producers. About 300 tonnes (330 tons) of gold are mined every year.

Southern states

Three regions characterize the 14 southern states: the Appalachian Mountains in the centre, the fertile plains of the south and west, and the tropical Gulf of Mexico. The states' mixed fortunes were established in the 19th century by cotton plantations worked by African slaves. Now, the region has a prosperous and varied economy that runs on farming, oil, coal, manufacturing, and tourism. Many people are devout Christians.

Mouthpiece with single reed

Jazz
Originating in New Orleans around the beginning of the 20th century, jazz music developed from the ragtime style played by black musicians at funerals and street parades. It gradually spread north to Chicago and New York City. The "Original Dixieland Jazz Band", a group of white musicians, were the first band to make jazz recordings.

New Orleans
Founded by the French in 1718, New Orleans is a major port and one of the largest metropolitan areas in the south, home to more than 500,000 people. Half are African Americans, but French influences remain, notably in the vibrant Mardi Gras (Shrove Tuesday) Festival.

Cotton
The USA is the world's second largest producer of cotton, most of which grows in the south. Founded in the days of slavery, the cotton industry is now highly mechanized and large-scale. The cotton fabric is used to make towels, sheets, and clothes. Denim is woven to make jeans.

Denim jeans

Disney World
One of America's top attractions, with more than 20,000,000 visitors a year, Walt Disney World opened in Orlando, Florida in 1971. The fantasy complex based on cartoon characters is a myriad of colour and music in a world of hotels and restaurants. The nearby Epcot Center exhibits future technology.

Jazz saxophone is accompanied by drums, piano, and double bass.

Farming
The southern states grow soya beans, tobacco, and half the country's supply of peanuts, much of which is used to make peanut butter. Florida is the world's second largest orange grower, and produces 75 per cent of the nation's supply.

Peanut butter

Peanuts

Southwestern states

Made wealthy by the discovery of oil, the six southwestern states share an arid landscape including part of the Rockies. Close links with Latin America have given this area the largest concentration of Native Americans in the USA, as well as many people of Spanish and *mestizo* descent. Houston, in Texas, is America's fourth largest city, and is the centre of the US space programme.

Navajo people

About 150,000 Navajos live in Arizona, Utah, and New Mexico on America's largest Native American reservation, which covers 70,000 sq km (24,000 sq miles). Formerly a nomadic people, Navajos are farmers, growing maize, beans, and squashes. They are skilled potters, weavers, and silversmiths.

Distinctive Navajo geometric design.

Navajo rug

Beef

Cattle ranching began in the mid-19th century to meet the food demands of growing cities on the east coast. Today, it is still a successful business, and cattle are raised on the vast plains throughout Texas, New Mexico, and eastern Colorado.

Oil workers use a horizontal drilling method.

Las Vegas

Filled with glittering neon signs that lure people into nightclubs and casinos, Las Vegas is an opulent urban creation devoted to gambling. Situated near the Grand Canyon, in the middle of Nevada's desert, Las Vegas attracts about 30 million visitors every year.

Oil industry

Since the discovery of oil in 1901, Texas has become America's top oil producer, alongside Alaska. One of the country's wealthiest cities, Houston is the heart of the industry, with its vast refineries.

Pacific states

The three states of Washington, Oregon, and California have a long Pacific coastline. The scenery varies from the mountains, volcanoes, and forests of the north, to the arid desert and Sierra Nevada range of California. All three states enjoy thriving economies. California is the most populated and attracts many tourists.

Logging

One-third of America's softwood comes from the vast cedar and fir forests of Oregon and Washington. Most is used to make paper. The world's tallest living trees are California's coast redwoods, growing up to 111 m (363 ft).

Hollywood

Home to many famous film stars, and a major centre of production, Hollywood, a suburb of Los Angeles, nestles in pretty, natural scenery. From the 1920s onwards, many major studios were established, and the area gained its glamourous reputation during the cinema heyday of the 1940s and 1950s. Many studios have now moved, but Hollywood remains the film capital of the world.

Three-strip Technicolor camera

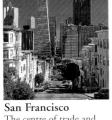

San Francisco

The centre of trade and shipping for the west coast, San Francisco lies on a natural bay. The hilly, green city endures frequent earthquakes, but its skyscrapers are built to withstand them. About six million people have made San Francisco and its suburbs their home.

CD

Silicon Valley

The Santa Clara Valley, south of San Francisco, has been dubbed "Silicon Valley", because more than 3,000 computer and other electronic firms are based there. It is a centre of high-tech innovation and thrives on the development of new ideas, often working in partnership with nearby Stanford University.

Avocado   **Grapes**   **Almonds**

Peach

Farming

Fertile soils and a warm climate enable California to produce about half of all America's fruit and vegetables, including avocados, peaches, and almonds. One-third of the country's apples are grown in Washington, but the main crop is grapes.

Alaska

Lying beyond Canada in northwestern North America, Alaska was bought from Russia in 1867. It is the largest of the states, and much of it is forest or snowy tundra with long, dark winter days. The oil discovery in 1968 made it one of the USA's greatest assets, and oil drilling, fishing, and forestry are the main activities. The population is sparse, but many Inuit still live there.

Hawaii

This chain of eight volcanic islands and 124 islets in the Pacific Ocean became the USA's 50th state in 1959. Palmed beaches have earned Hawaii a reputation as a tropical paradise, and tourism, with income from farming and US military bases, is the main earner. Most Hawaiians descend from Polynesian, European, American, Chinese, and Japanese immigrants.

FIND OUT MORE   DISNEY, WALT   EARTHQUAKES   FARMING   FILMS AND FILM-MAKING   FORESTS   JAZZ   LAKES   NATIVE AMERICANS   NEWSPAPERS AND MAGAZINES   NORTH AMERICA, HISTORY OF   OIL

UNITED STATES, HISTORY OF

JUST OVER 200 YEARS AGO, the British colonies on the east coast of America became the first colonies in the world to achieve independence from European rule. Within 100 years, they had created a nation that spanned the continent. Many Americans trekked westwards to settle on the prairies; others headed for California in search of gold. Millions of people came to America from Europe to escape poverty and persecution and begin a new life. Today, the United States is the world's richest nation, its people drawn from all over the globe.

Declaration of Independence, 1776

Birth of a nation

The 13 British colonies on the east coast of America resented paying high taxes without being represented in the British parliament. In 1775, colonists rose up against Britain. The next year the 13 colonies declared their independence. After five years of fighting, they forced the British to surrender in 1781.

US Constitution
In 1787, representatives of the American states drew up a constitution. They set up a federal system, sharing power between the states and central government.

Wagon trails

In 1862, the US government passed the Homestead Act, which gave farmers 65 hectares (160 acres) of land west of the Mississippi after they had cultivated it for five years. People headed for the plains in covered wagons. Some took the Oregon Trail over the Rockies to the northwest; others went south to California.

Waterproof canvas held up by iron hoops

Wooden wheel with iron rim

Wagon contained everything a family needed.

Expanding nation
Within 65 years of independence, the 13 original states on the east coast had expanded the territory of the USA across the whole continent.

	1776
	1783
	1803
	1845
	1846
	1848

Expansion of the United States

Wooden frame houses

Shanty towns
In order to exploit the mineral wealth of the country, workers lived in shanty towns around the mines. In 1848, gold was discovered in California, and many thousands of prospectors arrived in the area.

Coast to coast
Until the 1860s, most of the railways were in the eastern part of the country, and the only way to travel west was on horseback or by covered wagon. On 10 July 1869, the first transcontinental railway was completed, linking the two coasts together for the first time. Six further transcontinental railways were completed by 1909.

Immigration
Irish fleeing famine, Jews fleeing persecution, Italians and others fleeing poverty – all made their way across the Atlantic Ocean to start a new life in the USA. In one decade – the 1890s – the total population rose by 13 million to 76 million people. By 1907, more than 1 million people were arriving in the country each year from Europe. The USA became a melting pot of different languages and cultures.

Immigrants arrive in New York

Gettysburg

In 1861, civil war broke out between the northern and southern states over the issue of slavery. Fighting lasted for four years. One of the turning points was the Battle of Gettysburg in July 1863. At Gettysburg, the northward advance of the southern army was finally halted in a battle in which thousands lost their lives. The north eventually won the war, ensuring the abolition of slavery.

North and South clash at Gettysburg

Timeline

1783 United States of America is founded.

1787 Constitution of the USA is drawn up.

1789 George Washington is elected first president of the USA.

1861-65 Civil war between southern and northern states.

1890s USA becomes major industrialised power.

1903 President Roosevelt acquires right to build Panama Canal.

Theodore Roosevelt

U

Model T Ford was the first mass-produced vehicle.

Industrialization

Between 1870 and 1914, industrial output in the USA trebled, making it a powerful economy. In 1912, Henry Ford introduced mass production into the car industry.

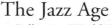

The Jazz Age

Following World War I, the American economy boomed. The 1920s became known as the Jazz Age, after the music of the time. In 1920, the American government introduced Prohibition – a ban on alcohol. Crime rose as gangsters fought for control of the alcohol trade.

Women's fashion of the early 1930s

Great Depression

In 1929, the New York Stock Exchange collapsed, causing a massive economic depression. By 1932, over 12 million Americans were out of work; soup kitchens were set up to feed the hungry.

Pearl Harbor

When war broke out in Europe in 1939, the USA stayed neutral. But on 7 December 1941, Japanese aircraft bombed the US fleet at anchor in Pearl Harbor, Hawaii. The USA joined the war against Germany, Italy, and Japan, fighting on many continents until victory in 1945.

JF Kennedy

Born in Massachusetts, John F. Kennedy (1917–63) was the 35th US President. He took office at the age of 43 – the youngest man to do so. His youth and vigour attracted many people, but he faced enormous problems. At home, he tried to tackle racial discrimination, as black Americans demanded the same rights as whites. Abroad he faced the threat of Soviet nuclear missiles in Cuba, which were removed after a tense period of negotiations in October 1962. Before completing his reforms, Kennedy was assassinated in Dallas, Texas.

Vietnam War

Between 1965 and 1973, Americans fought in South Vietnam in an attempt to prevent the unification of the country under communist North Vietnamese control.

Postwar society

Between 1945 and 1970, American science and industry flourished. The US economy quadrupled, and the real income of the average family doubled. Today, the nation is still a major power politically and economically, and is a world leader in technology and space research. However, this success does not extend to the whole population. Many cities suffer from mass unemployment and sub-standard housing, and many millions of Americans live in conditions of near poverty.

The 1950s

The 1950s were a period of rising wealth. Car ownership became common, and most families could afford to equip their homes with new electric appliances, such as washing machines.

Consumerism

In the 1950s, shopping malls opened across the country as rising prosperity allowed people to spend more on consumer goods. Many Americans were also able to take holidays abroad for the first time.

Woodstock

In the 1960s a new youth culture grew up based on rock music and, later, peaceful protests against the Vietnam War. More than 300,000 people, known as "hippies", went to the Woodstock music festival in 1969, one of the most successful music events of all time.

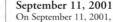

Wall Street

During the 1980s, the USA continued to prosper, and many people became wealthy by investing on Wall Street. But in 1987, the stock market crashed, wiping $500 billion off share values in a single day. Irresponsible trading was blamed for the disaster.

September 11, 2001

On September 11, 2001, the worst terrorist attack in history took place in the USA. Terrorists flew a hijacked passenger plane into the World Trade Center in New York City, resulting in an explosion that demolished its twin towers and killed almost 3,000 people. Other synchronized attacks on the day included a plane flown into the Pentagon in Washington, D.C. The USA retaliated with the bombing of Afghanistan, believed to harbour the key perpetrators of the crime, including the head of al-Qaida, Osama bin Laden.

Firemen battled bravely to find survivors.

1917 The USA enters World War I allied with Britain and France.

1920–33 Prohibition laws ban the sale and making of alcohol in the US.

1929 Wall Street Stock Exchange crashes in New York.

1929–39 Great Depression causes mass poverty

News of Wall St crash

1933 President FD Roosevelt promises a "New Deal" to get the USA out of the economic slump.

1945 The USA drops atomic bombs on Japan, ending World War II.

1945–89 "Cold War" between USA and Soviet Union.

1954 Supreme Court prohibits racial segregation in schools.

1965–73 Over 50,000 US troops killed in Vietnam.

1960s and 1970s Black people fight for equal rights.

1969 American Neil Armstrong is the first person on the Moon.

Ronald Reagan and Mikhail Gorbachev

1987 Presidents Reagan and Gorbachev sign the Nuclear Forces Treaty.

1991 Operation Desert Storm is launched against Iraq in the Gulf War.

2001 Terrorist attacks in the USA lead to the bombing of Afghanistan.

2003 US-led coalition deposes Saddam Hussein's regime in Iraq.

FIND OUT MORE   AMERICAN CIVIL WAR   AMERICAN REVOLUTION   COLD WAR   GREAT DEPRESSION   KING, MARTIN LUTHER   NORTH AMERICA, HISTORY OF   PILGRIM FATHERS   TRADE AND INDUSTRY

UNIVERSE

EVERYTHING THAT EXISTS makes up the Universe, from the smallest particles to the biggest structures, whether on Earth or in space. It includes everything that is visible, much that is invisible, everything that is known, and more that is unknown. Over time, humans have had different ideas of what the Universe is and how it works, how it started, and what its future is. Today, scientists know more than ever before, but there is much still to be learnt.

Structure of the Universe

The most common object in the Universe is the star. There are billions and billions of them. At least one of these, the Sun, has planets. One of these planets, Earth, has life. On the face of it stars, planets, and humans are very different, but they do have things in common. They are all made of the same chemical elements, or compounds of them, and they are all affected by the laws of science, such as gravity and the electromagnetic force. By studying the constituents of the Universe and understanding the laws, scientists can build up a picture of the Universe, and discover its past and predict its future.

Interstellar material
Gas and dust are found in the vast spaces between stars and make up about 10 per cent of the Universe. In places, the gas and dust is so thinly spread that it is like a vacuum; in other places, they make enormous clouds. Gas and dust can form new stars and be replenished by material from dying stars. Gas and dust are also found between the galaxies.

Great Wall
The largest structures in the Universe are long thread-like filaments made of thousands of galaxies. They surround huge, empty voids. Here a computer simulation shows the view from an imaginary spacecraft travelling above one such filament, known as the Great Wall.

The Universe was created 15 billion years ago in the Big Bang. Since then, matter has come together to form stars, galaxies, planets, and life.

A large star dies as a supernova.

Galaxies contain billions of stars.

The Sun, an ordinary middle-aged star

Clusters of stars

Cloud of gas and dust

Comet

Planets – balls of rock, gas, or ice

Real position of star

Apparent position of star

Path of light rays

Ptolemy
Once the Earth was thought to be the centre of the Universe with the other celestial objects moving around it. This idea is the Ptolemaic view, named after Claudius Ptolemy, an Egyptian. In the 2nd century AD, he brought together the astronomical ideas of the ancient Greek world in his work, the *Almagest*.

Dark matter
Scientists have calculated how much material the Universe contains: the answer is about 90 per cent more than has been detected. This gas cloud, with a cluster of galaxies embedded in it, may contain some of the missing material.

Gravity
A star's gas is held together by gravity. Everything in the Universe is affected by gravity. Earth's gravity keep things on its surface, the Sun's gravity keeps the Solar System together, and the stars in the Milky Way are held together by gravity. In general, the more massive a body is, the more gravitational pull it has.

General relativity
Early in the 20th century, gravity was shown to affect not only objects but space itself. Massive objects, which have immense gravitational pull, curve space. This pull is seen when the light from a star, instead of following a straight path through space, falls into the curved space created by the Sun. This law is called the general theory of relativity.

Looking at the Universe

Everything known about the Universe has been learnt from Earth or close to it. Telescopes collect information by picking up electromagnetic radiation, transmitted in a range of wavelengths, by every object in the Universe. By analysing different wavelengths, it is possible to build up a picture of the Universe.

Each wavelength gives different information about an object.

Infrared
Andromeda Galaxy as recorded at infrared wavelengths. Infrared images can help astronomers locate cooler objects and regions not visible at optical wavelengths.

Visible light
The Andromeda Galaxy at optical wavelengths. It is the largest of the galaxies close to the Milky Way. It has two smaller companion galaxies, also visible in this image.

X-rays
An X-ray image of the Andromeda Galaxy. X-rays are short wavelengths with high energy. They pinpoint "hot spots" or areas of intense activity in space.

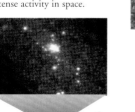

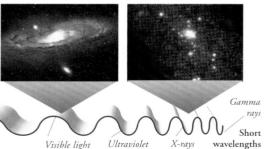

Edge of the Universe
As telescopes have improved, astronomers have been able to see farther and farther. With present instruments, they can see almost to the edge of the Universe, 15 billion light years away. This quasar, one of the most distant objects visible, is 12 billion light years away.

Long wavelengths

Radio waves   *Microwaves*   *Infrared*   *Visible light*   *Ultraviolet*   *X-rays*   *Gamma rays*   **Short wavelengths**